"Now is the time for women to empower themselves, with a healthy body, mind, and spirit. The time-tested tools of nutrition, meditation, yoga and breathing provided in this book have helped millions of people worldwide. Empowered we can come together in celebration and in service to each other and make the world a better place for all."

Sri Sri Ravi Shankar, Founder, The Art of Living Foundation

"Theresa and Susan are two remarkable women who most definitely practice what they preach... I have seen firsthand the impact both Theresa and Susan have had on so many people; their dedication to health, fitness and empowering women is an inspiration to so many. I am so pleased they have written another book which is sure to change lives for the better."

Erin Smith, Programs Manager, YMCA of Greater Toronto

"This holistic approach is the perfect tool to teach women that loving themselves inside and out is the key to a healthy life."

Erin Willson, Canadian Olympic Team Member - synchronized swimming

"This powerful, informative book offers women of all ages a roadmap to a healthy, balanced life. It's the perfect guide to releasing self-neglect and learning to love yourself in every way."

Patricia Sands, award-winning Canadian author

Also by Susan Sommers...

Marketing to Win: Creating and Sustaining Your Non-Profit
Building Media Relationships: How to Establish, Develop, and Maintain Long-Term Relationships with the Media

Also by Susan Sommers and Theresa Dugwell...

Power Source for Women: Proven Fitness Strategies, Tools, and Success Stories for Women 45+

LOVE

YOUR BODY...
EMBRACE YOUR

LIFE!

Susan Sommers & Theresa Dugwell

Co-authors of *Power Source for Women: Proven Fitness Strategies, Tools, and Success Stories for Women 45+*

BALBOA.
PRESS
A DIVISION OF HAY HOUSE

Balboa Press books may be ordered through booksellers or by contacting:

Balboa Press
A Division of Hay House
1663 Liberty Drive
Bloomington, IN 47403
www.balboapress.com
1 (877) 407-4847

Because of the dynamic nature of the Internet, any web addresses or links contained in this book may have changed since publication and may no longer be valid. The views expressed in this work are solely those of the author and do not necessarily reflect the views of the publisher, and the publisher hereby disclaims any responsibility for them.

The author of this book does not dispense medical advice or prescribe the use of any technique as a form of treatment for physical, emotional, or medical problems without the advice of a physician, either directly or indirectly. The intent of the author is only to offer information of a general nature to help you in your quest for emotional and spiritual well-being. In the event you use any of the information in this book for yourself, which is your constitutional right, the author and the publisher assume no responsibility for your actions.

Any people depicted in stock imagery provided by Thinkstock are models, and such images are being used for illustrative purposes only. Certain stock imagery © Thinkstock.

Print information available on the last page.

ISBN: 978-1-5043-5372-4 (sc)
ISBN: 978-1-5043-5373-1 (e)

Balboa Press rev. date: 05/27/2016

This book is dedicated to...

...All of the women and girls in my life, but above all – to my mother, Lee Sommers, for encouraging me, believing in me, and inspiring me. In my mind and my heart, you will always be my role model.

Susan Sommers

...My niece, Brianna. You are growing into an incredible young lady. What makes you even more amazing is that you know the importance of believing in yourself and loving who you are. You are a shining example of the spirit of this book at only fourteen years of age – you are an inspiration to so many girls and the brightest light in my life.

Theresa Dugwell

Contents

Preface

Our new book *LOVE YOUR BODY... Embrace Your Life!* is designed to promote self-awareness and to build self-acceptance, self-esteem, and self-love in women of all ages, backgrounds, and stages of life. The book shows women how to nurture self-compassion: to get started, stay motivated, and reap the rewards of a solid relationship with their mind and body. In addition, we offer the latest research findings, quizzes, strategies, tools, and action plans for women to strengthen their mental, emotional, physical, and spiritual well-being.

Our own **FIT Motivational Styles**, accomplishments, goals, and lifestyles have changed since we wrote *Power Source for Women: Proven Fitness Strategies, Tools, and Success Stories for Women 45+.*[1] We wanted to update our stories in this new book.

Prior to 2010, Theresa Dugwell had completed over twenty full marathons. Since then, she set three Guinness World Records for running the greatest distance in twelve hours on a treadmill in the overall category and the women's category. She is currently training to try out in the masters provincial qualifying races in the 100-meter distance. She has also become a certified spinning instructor and fitness instructor.

Since 2003, Susan Sommers has completed thirty-three races, including two full marathons at ages sixty-one and sixty-three. Since 2010, she has expanded her health and fitness program to include weight-training workouts, lap swimming, stretching, and meditation. She continues to complete several half-marathons and 5K races each year.

Background

LOVE YOUR BODY...Embrace Your Life! evolved from the physical, mental, and emotional strategies and tools highlighted in our first book, *Power Source for Women: Proven Fitness Strategies, Tools, and Success Stories for Women 45+.* Based on the responses to our first book, we decided to expand the contents of the new book to include sections on self-compassion, self-love, spirituality, and nutrition, created by experts in these fields:

Debra Joy Eklove, BCom, MSc, CAE, and **Nayna Trehan**, BCom – The Art of Living Foundation (AOLF), a non-profit educational and humanitarian organization founded in 1981 by the world-renowned philanthropist and spiritual leader, Sri Sri Ravi Shankar, with chapters in 152 countries around the world

Kirsten Bedard, BSc Nutrition, ACE – one of Canada's most knowledgeable nutrition and exercise coaches, founder of Ladylean, and author of *Read This Before You Diet*[2]

Catherine M. Sabiston, PhD, Canada Research Chair in Physical Activity and Mental Health, Associate Professor, Faculty of Kinesiology and Physical Education, University of Toronto, and **Eva Pila**, MSc, PhD candidate, Exercise Sciences, University of Toronto – conducting groundbreaking studies on girls' and women's self-compassion, self-esteem, and self-love

As we became more motivated and committed to health and fitness over the past fifteen years, we looked for new **role models**, women who had achieved incredible things at different ages and stages of life. Through their stories, we have gained more information on ways to embrace and care for our bodies as we age. With their inspiring quotes throughout this book, we have included four of our role models in this book, women who have inspired us on our own journeys:

Olga Kotelko, lived to age 95 – Competed in high jump, long jump, triple jump, shot put, javelin, hammer and discus throws and the 100-meter, 200-meter and 400-meter sprints. One of Canada's most accomplished athletes held twenty-six world records in her age category. She was the author of *The O.K. Way to a Healthy and Happy Life*,[3] and the subject of *What Makes Olga Run? The Mystery of the 90-Something Track Star and What She Can Teach Us About Living Longer, Happier Lives* by Bruce Grierson.[4] Olga died in June 2014 after setting seven new records a few months before her death.

Jessamyn Stanley, 27 – "Fat femme" yogi and Instagram sensation with 29,000 followers. This plus-size model posts videos and photos of her non-traditional body in yoga poses on Instagram. She often focuses on complex poses like advanced inversions to prove that a person's size should not prevent him or her from practicing yoga. She plans to launch a crowd funding campaign to pay for her training to be a certified yoga instructor.

Kathrine Switzer, 68 – The first woman to officially enter the Boston Marathon (in 1967), she led the drive to get the women's marathon into the Olympic Games (1984). She was inducted into the National Women's Hall of Fame in 2011. Kathrine Switzer is the author of *Marathon Woman* and *Running and Walking for Women Over 40*, and co-author of the book, *26.2 Marathon Stories.*[5]

Margaret Webb, 51 – Toronto-based Margaret Webb has had an exciting twenty-five year writing career that includes stints as a non-fiction author, magazine editor and writer, journalist, fiction writer, screenwriter for film and TV, playwright and poet. She co-wrote the feature film *Margarita*, which hit theatres in 2012, became a popular indie romantic comedy on Netflix in 2014 and has played at some 100 film festivals around the world, garnering nine awards. She is the author of the best-selling book *Older, Faster, Stronger,*[6] about her own journey to get stronger, faster, and happier after fifty, through her own running and the stories of trailblazing pioneers of women's running.

New interactive tools were created for this book, including our **FIT Motivational Ladder**, our **FIT Workbook and Gratitude Journal**, our **Weekly FIT Training Log**, and our **vision board** and **photography** sections. Our **expanded website**, www.powersourceforwomen.com, includes an online community where women can connect with other women, exchange ideas, ask questions, submit success stories, contribute blog posts, and access professional coaching in health, nutrition, and fitness.

Our Goals

- To redefine success and to encourage women to live the life they truly want and deserve
- To change the way women talk to (and about) their bodies, to themselves and to others, no matter where they are on their journey
- To encourage women to spend time patiently listening to their bodies, to gain the information they need for a personal transformation
- To motivate women to shape their lives from the inside out, to stay "inner driven"
- To encourage women to practice self-compassion and to nurture self-awareness, self-acceptance, and self-love
- To suggest ways for women to focus on the beauty within themselves and in others, including their good qualities, kindness, gifts, and talents
- To inspire women to create daily tools, techniques, habits, practices, and plans that work for their unique bodies and needs
- To motivate women to discover and embrace their unique strengths and skills, at every stage of their lives

- To introduce our role models, women from twenty-seven to ninety-five who are helping to change women's attitudes towards their bodies and body image, online and offline
- To showcase our partners and to highlight the organizations and companies that are altering women's perceptions about health, fitness, spirituality, and their bodies
- To offer an online community where women can connect with other women, exchange ideas, ask questions, submit their success stories, contribute blog posts, and access professional coaching in nutrition, fitness, and mental health
- To provide a new Facebook page, where women and girls can connect with each other and with the co-authors
- To raise awareness, support, and understanding for vitiligo, a skin pigment condition that has been part of Theresa Dugwell's life since she was sixteen

There's no time like the present to begin to nurture yourself. Take the opportunity, as you travel through our book, to think beyond where you are today. Learn about yourself and explore the information you find here. Move through this book with an open mind and be inspired. You have one life and if you aren't feeling great right now, it's time for a change. It's true that a deep sense of satisfaction can come from caring for others and ensuring that their needs are met. But remember, time does not stand still. Start to nurture yourself today. Tap into your capacity for greatness.

Welcome. We are glad you are here!
Susan Sommers and Theresa Dugwell, 2016

Acknowledgments

Susan Sommers' Acknowledgments

First of all, I'd like to thank Theresa Dugwell for collaborating with me on two books: *Power Source for Women: Proven Fitness Strategies, Tools, and Success Stories for Women 45+* and *LOVE YOUR BODY... Embrace Your Life!* It has been a labor of love and such a pleasure working with you. Thanks to my husband, Peter, for meeting me during my marathons and half-marathons to talk me across the finish line (and carry my bag and jacket).

My thanks to my family: my late mother Lee and father Harry, who taught me about fitness at a young age and inspired me to exercise; to my two daughters, Andrea and Danielle, and their husbands, Eric and Allan for cheering me on; and to my brother, Howard; my step-daughter, Kellie Keyes and her husband, Danny. Thanks to my California family and to my grandchildren, nieces, and nephews.

And a special thanks to my trainers, Chen Cohen (my first marathon), Beverly Tyler (my second marathon), and Joanne Fontana (my new fitness program).

Theresa Dugwell's Acknowledgments

I want to acknowledge every woman who has ever entered into my life. It is because of you I have learned so much about the many seasons we go through as females. From the curious little girl, to the inspired young lady, and then to the enlightened woman who becomes a source of energy for so many – it is because of you I am able to write this book with my incredibly talented co-author Susan.

Introduction

Our Stories

Susan Sommers' Story

Growing up in the suburbs of New Jersey, I was introduced to a number of sports as a child. My father taught my older brother and me how to roller skate, ice skate, swim, bowl, and bike.

I now realize that my father was at the forefront of the home gym movement. In the 1950s, he set up a rowing machine, a chinning bar, and hand weights in the basement of our house. My brother, Howard, was recovering from polio and my father exercised with him. However, as a girl in that traditional decade, I was not encouraged to try the machines and the weights. In fact, it took me another forty years to commit to weights and strength training.

I was quite short and always loved candy and cookies. From the time I was ten until I started to smoke at the age of sixteen, I was self-conscious about my weight and my body. I tried to be noticed as the girl with the great sense of humor. For the next twenty years, I controlled my weight through a combination of tools, including smoking, dieting, and diet pills.

My mother and her two sisters were also obsessed with weight – their own and that of their three daughters. When I went away to university, I took a black coat with me: whenever I gained weight, I wore it when I got off the plane to meet my mother. That coat became a symbol for self-consciousness about my body.

In 1980, I divorced, stopped smoking cold turkey, and immediately gained weight. In addition, I started my own public relations firm in 1982, which added to my stress. For the next fifteen years, I tried to change my body through a combination of aerobics classes, swimming, skipping meals, and yo-yo dieting – with little success.

The Turning Point

As I entered my fifties and menopause, I knew I had to change my eating habits. I wanted to find healthier ways to handle stress and relax. I was also tired of years I spent weight cycling.

When I started to work full time as a marketing coach at the YMCA business center in 2002, I received two free YMCA annual fitness memberships – one for my husband, Peter, and one for me. At fifty-eight, I attended my first Saturday run fit class and started to slowly walk and jog. After that class, walking, slow jogging, and weight training became my passions. I decided to challenge myself and took my first step by entering a 5K race at the age of fifty-nine. I won first prize in my age category – a pair of socks and a certificate!

Since 2003, I have completed over thirty races – including two full marathons, which involved seven and a half hours of walking. When I completed the marathons, I realized that I had never given my body credit for all of the things it had achieved, and I truly celebrated my successes.

During that time, I also watched my mother fight chronic pain and gradually lose her mobility due to osteoarthritis. When she died in early 2009 from Alzheimer's disease, she was bedridden.

This gave me an added incentive to keep moving. I vowed I would increase my core strength and flexibility through a fitness program that I could sustain as I aged. Today, I have achieved improved health through a manageable program of moderate weight training, walking, jogging, swimming, and stretching. I also incorporated guided meditation into my daily life. Along the way, I have transformed my body and my health.

Today, I am proud of the way I look and feel.

Theresa Dugwell's Story

I grew up with a single mom and two younger siblings in the city of Toronto. Being the eldest, I sometimes took on the role of a little mom looking out for my younger sisters to help my mother. I had to grow up fast and take on responsibilities because that was needed in our family, especially during the times that my mom needed a break.

The challenges I faced as a young girl, I believe, were a bit more difficult for me because I did not have a strong father figure present when times got tough. I remember being bullied at twelve years of age, and for one year I ran back and forth from school and hid out just to stay safe.

Then at sixteen years of age I developed a skin disorder called vitiligo. At the time I was devastated. My body was attacking its own melanocytes and slowly causing my skin color to disappear and turn into white patches that covered my body.

Both situations created enormous stress, and I felt alone and afraid.

The Turning Point

Though I did not realize it at the time, the onset of vitiligo at sixteen was a pivotal moment in my life. Looking at the stressors that showed up for me in the early years, I was prompted to take a keen interest in understanding my health and building a strong mind and body. I began to research all kinds of health books so I could learn about my body and the vitiligo. I started to learn the importance of health through nutrition and exercise. When I felt stressed I would close my bedroom door, turn on the music, and exercise. Whenever I did this I felt so much better and I would not obsess over my skin condition. I would be a much happier young girl.

Today I continue on the journey of exercise to feel good about myself and to take care of my mind and body. It is my number one priority because it is my life force and it fuels my energy for everything else.

When I look back at the challenges of growing up with a single mom and two younger sisters, struggling sometimes just to get by,

I commend my amazing mother for the bravery that it took to raise three little girls. Today I believe I am a stronger woman because of what I learned from my mother just by watching her.

My health and fitness are what fuel me with energy and make me a better person. I have been fortunate to have achieved some wonderful physical feats. Today I hold three Guinness World Records for running the greatest distance on a treadmill in twelve hours and I have completed twenty-one marathons – each one a challenge and each one a celebration of what is possible.

Our Story Together

We met in the summer of 2007 at a Toronto YMCA, where we were both members. We talked about all of the wonderful women we saw, from twenty-two to ninety years of age, working out at six in the morning, and we wanted to show how they could motivate and inspire other women to commit to their health and fitness.

In the fall of 2007, Theresa created the YMCA Women's Workshop Series, "Celebrating Our Women," to give these women an opportunity to develop their stories into a presentation. The workshops were designed to educate, motivate, and build community.

Susan was the first speaker in October 2007, shortly after completing her second marathon at the age of sixty-three. Subsequently, eight other women were invited to tell their stories and to share their successes and challenges.

The wonderful outcome of this experience was that women found inspiration and were eager to learn more. As other women heard about the events, they contacted us for advice and motivation. As a result, in the fall of 2009, we decided to write a book that would include health and fitness strategies, tools, and success stories for women. In September 2010, we launched our book *Power Source for Women: Proven Fitness Strategies, Tools, and Success Stories for Women 45+* in Los Angeles and Toronto. Over the next four years, we were busy with speaking engagements, consumer shows, travel, and our own businesses.

Our Story Today

Our own lives, goals, and motivations have changed dramatically since we wrote *Power Source for Women: Proven Fitness Strategies, Tools, and Success Stories for Women 45+.* Our own **FIT Motivational Styles**, lifestyles, and accomplishments have also changed.

Prior to 2010, Theresa Dugwell completed over twenty full marathons. Since then, she set three Guinness World Records for running the greatest distance in twelve hours on a treadmill in the overall category and the women's category. She is currently training to try out in the masters provincial qualifying races in the 100-meter distance. She has also become a certified spinning instructor and fitness instructor.

Prior to 2010, Susan Sommers had completed twenty-seven races, including two full marathons at sixty-one and sixty-three – all walking and slow jogging. Since 2010, she has completed six new races, including half-marathons, 10K, and 5K races. She has also expanded her health and fitness program to include weight-training workouts, distance swimming, stretching, and meditation.

Believe in Yourself

"I'm not afraid of my body. I'm not afraid to see every awkward curve or strange way it can look. I'm willing to be in my underwear upside down."

Jessamyn Stanley, 27

Seven trends that show how women and girls today are making commitments to their own mental, physical, emotional, and spiritual health:

1. **Groundbreaking new research on self-compassion, body image, health, and fitness**
   This work is being conducted at universities and organizations around the world. In our book, we are grateful to have contributions by the University of Toronto's Catherine M. Sabiston and Eva Pila. Dr. Sabiston is a Canada Research Chair in Physical Activity and Mental Health, and an associate professor in the Faculty of Kinesiology and Physical Education. Eva Pila is a PhD candidate at the university's Graduate Deparament of Exercise Science.

2. **Breathing, meditation, mindfulness, and yoga**
   Women of all ages are finding ways to connect to their spirituality, minds, and emotions, through breathing exercises,

meditation, mindfulness, and yoga. From their teens to their nineties, women everywhere are committing to their mental and spiritual health, alone and in groups. Worldwide, The Art of Living Foundation is at the forefront of this movement.

3. **New online tools and apps**
Facebook, Twitter, Instagram, and Pinterest are connecting women and girls around the world directly to women of all ages and sizes who embrace their bodies and celebrate themselves.

4. **Companies that are making a difference**
Through their powerful messaging and thought-provoking videos and ads, campaigns like the Dove Self-Esteem Project for girls and Nike ads remind women and girls how important it is to feel good about themselves – from the inside out.

5. **Fostering your support network**
Research shows that an essential ingredient of fitness success for women involves teaming up with other people who support and encourage them to reach their goals. Online and offline, it is important to build a network of people who will support you and keep you motivated in your commitment to health and fitness. Include your friends, sisters, mothers, daughters, and the men in your life. Keep in touch with them on a daily or weekly basis in person, by phone, through e-mail, on Facebook, or through Twitter or Skype.

6. **Daily fitness and functional workouts**
Experts agree that some type of physical activity or regular exercise on a daily basis is recommended for long-term fitness and health. Research shows that taking part in activities that keep you moving for a total of thirty to sixty minutes throughout the day can greatly benefit your health and well-being. Work towards a goal of 10,000 steps per day.

Simply adding movement into your daily routine can increase your level of fitness. For example, you can park in the last row of the parking lot and walk between your office and your car. You can walk up and down the stairs, walk the dog for ten minutes when you get home, get off the bus or subway several stops early and walk the extra distance, go mall walking, ride a bicycle, garden, mow the lawn, or shovel snow.

7. **Races and other competitions**

More than ever before, women and girls are entering competitions and races. Every body shape, fitness level, and age can be seen walking, biking, and running at events around the world. Often there are more women than men in these races! What a change from the time when one of our role models, Kathrine Switzer, was physically attacked mid-stride by a race director when she officially entered and ran in the Boston Marathon in 1967.

No Time Like the Present

As women, each day we get up and go about our normal routines. These usually involve many responsibilities, from caring for family or aging parents, to earning a living for our families and ourselves. Sometimes we're so consumed by life's demands, we don't notice that we're not nurturing ourselves, mentally, physically, and emotionally. Ask yourself two questions: Who am I – independent of my family, friends, work, and responsibilities? How am I taking care of myself?

Challenge Your Personal Barriers

You know the importance of being healthy and fit, but you also know the time and effort it requires. You may feel you don't have enough time for exercise, meditation, and eating healthy foods. Women face a long list of challenges and barriers. Check off the barriers that may apply to you. Then ask yourself, what is your motivation for reading our book and committing to physical, mental, emotional, and spiritual health?

- [ ] I'm too busy.
- [ ] I'm too tired.
- [ ] I don't have time.
- [ ] I have too much work.
- [ ] I'll never look like [insert a celeb name of your choice], so why bother?
- [ ] I can't afford the expensive equipment or the health club membership I need to get fit.
- [ ] Exercise is boring.
- [ ] I have arthritis or stiff joints.
- [ ] I don't like to work out.
- [ ] I'm too sore from my last workout.
- [ ] I'm getting sick.
- [ ] I feel guilty about taking the time for myself.
- [ ] I am unsteady on my feet.
- [ ] I'm afraid of falling.
- [ ] I have concerns about my heart.
- [ ] My friends and family don't support my efforts to work out.
- [ ] I'm too lazy.
- [ ] I'm self-conscious about how I look when I exercise.
- [ ] I'm not athletic.
- [ ] The young instructors intimidate me.
- [ ] I always quit.
- [ ] I'm too stressed.
- [ ] It's too cold.
- [ ] It's too dark.
- [ ] It will be too difficult.
- [ ] I can't allow myself to fail.
- [ ] I can't change.
- [ ] I'm too old.
- [ ] I'm too busy with work.

Olga Kotelko's Nine Rules to Remember[7]

1. Keep moving
Move constantly, even when you are not exercising.

2. **Create routines (but sometimes break them)**
   Committing the more mundane parts of our life to habits and routines frees up RAM for the things that matter to us.

3. **Be opportunistic**
   Spend your precious energy wisely. Conserve energy when you can, but when you need to go for it, go for it.

4. **Be a mensch**
   Doing good doesn't just feel good – it works. It's healthy for the tribe and healthy for us.

5. **Believe in something**
   Belief is a trait of temperament. People tend to thrive when they have a belief system and embrace life's puzzles as opportunities for problem solving.

6. **Lighten up**
   Managing stress is staggeringly important in terms of flipping genetic switches.

7. **Cultivate a sense of progress**
   According to studies of life satisfaction and human motivation, we all need to feel like we're improving. Identify your expectations, adjust them to allow for small wins, then improve upon them.

8. **Don't do it if you don't love it**
   People can't be guilted into lasting healthy behavior change. "Should" doesn't work.

9. **Begin now**
   Midlife is not too late to embark on this. Providing we rev up slowly, in some ways, it's the best time for it.

Introducing Our Ten-Step FIT Motivational Ladder™

As you progress through this book, you will be inspired to change your mind, change your body, and change your emotions. In the next chapters, we take you through an easy, ten-step process to achieve your goals.

PART 1

LOVE YOUR BODY

Love Your Body...

Embrace a strong, lifelong relationship with your mind, body, and spirit.

Think about how it feels when you are in a beautiful fulfilling relationship – the joy, excitement, and love you feel in your heart when you are connected with someone. All you see is what is perfect and wonderful; there are no flaws that you can see. You truly love and appreciate the other person for who they are. You have respect and trust for one another with a deep sense of inner peace that everything is okay. The possibilities are endless and you feel good about yourself.

But this book isn't about how good it is with your significant other. This book is about a relationship that is even more critical in your life; one that brings you the most joy and excitement when you are connected. This is the relationship you wake up to each morning and go to bed with every night. The one you cannot run or hide from or pretend you love. If you disrespect it and focus on what's not good about it, then your inner world will live in conflict. It must be nurtured like a flower. Feed it love and respect, and it will blossom into a beautiful relationship with you.

Your body needs you and you need your body.

Let's begin your journey loving the body you were born with and develop a loving relationship with yourself. You will explore all the possibilities in your life in the areas of health, fitness, and spirituality. This book is all for you. So let's get started loving your body and embracing your life!

How Women Learn About Beauty and Body Image

There are so many ways that women and girls are bombarded with images of beauty, and it is not surprising that they are often overwhelmed and insecure about their bodies and themselves. Here are some of the ways that "perfection" for women is promoted:

*   Television
*   Magazines
*   Books

- Newspapers
- Online media – websites, chat rooms, YouTube, Facebook, blogs, Twitter
- Celebrities
- Family members
- Significant others
- Friends and peers
- Bosses and co-workers
- Teachers
- Fitness centers, gyms, classes, and trainers
- Corporations – food, pharmaceutical, diet companies, and other product manufacturers
- Non-profit organizations
- The medical community and health care professionals
- Athletes, teams, and coaches
- Retailers
- Manufacturers
- Other men and women

Research-Based Strategies for Raising Girls With a Healthy Body Image

by Catherine M. Sabiston and Eva Pila

Raising girls with a healthy body image can be very challenging when there are widespread unrealistic standards about what the body should look like, and so much contradictory evidence for which lifestyle habits constitute as healthy. The social environment makes it all too easy for girls to develop preoccupations with their body, weight, food, and exercise.

As a mature female role model (and a mother, stepmother, grandmother, or aunt), you play a very important role in promoting balanced thoughts about food, exercise, body image, and overall self-worth. Based on the most recent research evidence, the following list provides some strategies for helping to raise girls with positive body image and self-esteem.

Be a role model of body appreciation, body acceptance, and self-love. Show compassion to yourself and your body as it naturally changes. As a mature female, you are the biggest role model for how your young girl will view her body and how her attitudes around food and exercise will be shaped.

Recognize that changes in weight and body shape are very common, especially in adolescence and young adulthood. Discussing natural body changes with a young girl will encourage important dialogue for her to accept her body as it grows.

Try to limit any comments or talk regarding weight, appearance, and diets. Some experts even recommend zero diet and weight talk about yourself, your young girl, or anyone else. Making a point not to discuss outer appearance and diets will teach girls that their bodies are more than something to be looked at. Even when complimenting or praising young girls – choose characteristics that are not associated with her appearance. For example, instead of stating, "You look very beautiful today," you could offer a compliment that focuses on a positive attribute such as, "You look very happy today."

Challenge your own weight-related biases and prejudices to help teach girls the importance of accepting and appreciating all shapes and sizes. Exposing her to diverse role models can help her appreciate all the qualities that women have to offer beyond appearance.

Teach her to be critical of the media and societal messages around placing value judgments on specific body types. Teach her how marketing strategies and photo manipulations can skew perceptions of what models look like.

Reflect with her on how body, weight, eating, and fitness are discussed within her friendship groups. Aside from you and other important mature females in her life, her peer groups will have the greatest influence on how she views her body.

Engage in family mealtimes that involve a large variety of food. It is helpful to involve her in the meal planning, grocery shopping, and cooking process. Teach her that all food can be enjoyed and that food is a very important part of many social and cultural activities. Rather than dichotomizing food into categories (e.g. good/healthy or bad/unhealthy) you could focus on the color of food by challenging her to come up with the most colorful plate of food during her meals.

Encourage her to engage in physical activities that she enjoys. Try different physical activities together – unstructured activities like playing with the family in the park, running around in the backyard, or going hiking with siblings. Offer choices for different activities whenever possible – this will help promote her motivation.

Help her dissociate eating and exercise from her weight and appearance. Teach her that nutrition and exercise should be enjoyable experiences that help nourish her body – and that weight and appearance should be appreciated on their own accord.

Recognize the girl as the expert of her own body's needs. Give her power to decide the types of foods and amounts she enjoys based on taste and nourishment – this will help her to develop intuitive eating patterns. Learning to listen to her body's cues for hunger and satiety will help her make nutrition choices that nourish her body and mind.

Acknowledge her as the best judge of her clothing, accessories, hairstyle, and general appearance. Encouraging her to pick the outfits she feels comfortable in will teach her the value of expressing herself in different ways. Rather than picking which outfits you believe flatter her most, empower her to choose based on her personal instincts.

Where Are You Now?

Take our FIT Lifestyle Quiz™

Select the **FIT Lifestyle** box for each question that best reflects the way you are living today. Be honest so you can clearly identify the areas where you need to achieve the greatest change.

FIT Lifestyle Quiz

	Never 0	Occasionally 1	Frequently 2	Always 3
I live by the motto: early to bed, early to rise	☐	☐	☐	☐
I get 7–9 hours of sleep most nights	☐	☐	☐	☐
I have a good social network	☐	☐	☐	☐
I am grateful for the things in my life	☐	☐	☐	☐
I have a hobby I enjoy	☐	☐	☐	☐
I set goals for myself	☐	☐	☐	☐
I like to spend time with friends and family	☐	☐	☐	☐
I set aside time just for me	☐	☐	☐	☐
I enjoy my work, in or out of the home	☐	☐	☐	☐
I have a close friend or partner with whom I can share my thoughts, goals, and frustrations	☐	☐	☐	☐
I like my body	☐	☐	☐	☐
I am happy	☐	☐	☐	☐
I exercise regularly	☐	☐	☐	☐

I enjoy outdoor activities	☐	☐	☐	☐
I have regular checkups with my doctor	☐	☐	☐	☐
I reward myself for achievements or goals reached	☐	☐	☐	☐
Most of my meals are well-balanced and prepared in a healthy manner	☐	☐	☐	☐
I try to drink 6–8 glasses of water every day	☐	☐	☐	☐
I take short breaks during the day for myself	☐	☐	☐	☐
I enjoy reading or listening to health-related topics on self-improvement	☐	☐	☐	☐
I am good at problem solving	☐	☐	☐	☐
I am optimistic about my future	☐	☐	☐	☐
I eat healthy foods and occasionally reward myself with a treat	☐	☐	☐	☐
I have healthy ways to deal with my stress, such as meditation	☐	☐	☐	☐
I take action if I am dissatisfied with something in my life	☐	☐	☐	☐

Calculating Your FIT Lifestyle Score

Add up your points. The point values (0–3) are located above the four different responses. Once you know your total, read below to see where you place on the **FIT Lifestyle Scale** and the course of action we suggest for you to achieve your **FIT Healthy Lifestyle**.

FIT Lifestyle Scale

Low 0–26	Average 27–53	Optimal 54–75

If You Scored 0–26 Points

It's time to take immediate action.

First of all, congratulations for completing this self-assessment quiz and especially for being honest. We believe you're reading this book because you really want to change things in your life and become healthier – physically, mentally, and spiritually. You are probably feeling the negative effects of your lifestyle, physically and mentally, on a daily basis. Your energy level may be very low, so it's difficult for you to get motivated to make changes. We are ready to give you guidance through the strategies, tools, and success stories in this book.

But we suggest you visit your doctor first to discuss your current health status and your goals, so you can move ahead on your journey to a better you. You want to make sure, as you travel through this book, that you can tap into the tools and start making changes. Get the go-ahead from your doctor and then start to move.

If You Scored 27–53 Points

Your lifestyle is okay, but it's time to make it better.

Your lifestyle could use some major changes. You have probably been feeling frustrated with yourself and somewhat stuck in a pattern you can't seem to change. Maybe it's all of the responsibilities that keep you moving, but you have little time to stop and think about your own needs.

Start by working on the aspects of your lifestyle where you answered "occasionally" and "never." You'll certainly discover the pay-off in your energy levels and sense of well-being by beginning with a few changes. Remember, one change at a time can add up fast.

If You Scored 54–75 Points

Your lifestyle looks good. Why not make it great?

You are a shining example of someone who is trying to be proactive about your health and your body, making choices that are good for you. You live a balanced lifestyle, but you may have a few areas you want to improve.

Well, here's your chance. Look over your responses and find the ones where you scored "occasionally" and "never." These are the areas that could use some attention. So get into action today and make the changes. Why not feel even better?

Tips for Healthy Living

With your **FIT Lifestyle Quiz** results in hand, we created fifteen healthy living tips to follow as you work towards building a healthier lifestyle.

1. Take stock of how you spend your day. Concentrate on the important things that need to get done and cut down on the unnecessary items. This will help you reduce your stress.
2. Create balance by engaging in moderate behavior in your eating, working, resting, playing, hobbies, and socializing.
3. Learn how to say no. Don't take on too many things. This can sometimes lead to unnecessary stress and burnout.
4. Identify something you love to do and find a way to fit it into your life.
5. Keep your life simple. Try to be less materialistic and enjoy the more basic things in life, such as long walks in the park and on nature trails.
6. What you think and how you think affects your general well-being. Try to stay away from negative or self-derogatory thoughts, emotions, and people. This will require practice, but that's okay. In time you will master a new skill and feel better about yourself.
7. Cultivate your spiritual side by keeping in touch with your intuition and your inner self.
8. Eat well and healthy. Buy a new cookbook or look online and try new recipes. Make meals interesting, colorful, and fun.
9. Exercise your eyes regularly, especially if you spend a lot of time in front of the computer.
10. Go for regular medical checkups. If you have health problems, talk to your doctor and discuss all of the options available to you.

11. Take an interest in other people and volunteer in your community.
12. Read books, listen to audio books, or watch videos on self-improvement or on a subject that interests you. Try to learn one new thing every day.
13. Watch comedies. A good laugh is great for your mind and body.
14. Start to pay attention to this moment – your now. Whatever you are doing at this time, do it well. Whatever you are thinking, keep an open mind and be curious.
15. When you have an opportunity to take a nap in the afternoon, go for it. It's a great way to refresh your brain.

What do you need to change, adapt, compromise, or reject in order to strengthen your relationship with your body and your body image?

Our Turn...

Introducing Four **FIT Motivational Tools**™

1. Write it

The **FIT Workbook and Gratitude Journal** is a secure online resource where you can share your thoughts and record information on your body, mind, activity, and well-being (www. powersourceforwoment.com).

Here in this book we've included some ideas and questions to get you started at the end of each step on the **FIT Motivational Ladder**. Think about them and create your own entries in your **FIT Workbook and Gratitude Journal**.

The **FIT Workbook and Gratitude Journal** offers a way to appreciate where you are now, and to pay attention to the good things, experiences, and people in your life. Develop your own daily appreciation habits. Use your **FIT Workbook and Gratitude Journal** as a reminder to stop, breathe, and take a moment to fully experience the emotion of gratitude.

Keep your gratitude journal to help you remember all the things that are good in your life. When you start feeling stressed, spend a few minutes looking through your notes to remind yourself what really matters.

Be kind to yourself! Kindness means opening your heart to the gentle qualities of caring and compassion. When it comes to self-kindness, you need to have reasonable expectations and give yourself due praise. In order to nurture the gentle quality of kindness, cherish yourself.

When you do something for yourself, you automatically extend that same energy to others. Kindness melts barriers and re-empowers people who are afraid. Reach out to people: the lonely, the shy, the isolated, and the sad. In turn you will have a sense of inner peace, warmth, and love.

Use the **FIT Workbook and Gratitude Journal** to enjoy good experiences like good health and a sun-filled day. Celebrate accomplishments like trying a new hobby or mastering a new task. Each day, appreciate yourself and your life. Acknowledge the good people and experiences in your life.

2. Visualize it

Design your own **vision board**. Vision boards offer you a chance to imagine, illustrate, and dream. Fill them with photos, captions, quotes, and words. Include magazine articles, blog posts, Pinterest posts, inspirational quotes, goals, and images of the future.

This is a powerful technique that can help clarify your goals, priorities, and dreams and can often reveal a strategy on how to accomplish them. Vision boards are being used increasingly in corporate and business environments for team building and leadership development as well. This magical tool can help you engage your imagination.

When putting your vision board together, try not to analyze or think too much about the images you've chosen. Don't try to be perfect. Just allow your right brain, your creative and imaginative side, free rein. Illustrate your dreams.

This process can often provide an authentic solution to a person's problem, even when that person is stuck. The psychological healing benefit of the vision board process is immense. It takes a person on an inner journey and gives them a creative roadmap.

What to include in your vision board:

- Images and words found in magazines or online
- Magazine articles
- Blog posts
- Pinterest posts
- Inspirational quotes
- A picture of yourself
- Affirmations, inspirational words, quotations, and thoughts

3. Snap it

Use photography to capture pictures of the types of places, things, and people that inspire your goals. These can include photos of your favorite place to run or meditate, a track you'd like to run on, or your goal weight to lift.

4. Connect with us

Connect on our expanded website www.powersourceforwomen.com. Our website features our **FIT Workbook and Gratitude Journal**. We've created a private place for women to record their feelings, thoughts, and ideas about their bodies, food, and fitness; share their stories; and display their vision boards.

Your Turn…

Some ideas to get you started:

1. Write in your **FIT Workbook and Gratitude Journal**.
    - What were your results in the **FIT Lifestyle Quiz**?

- What is your motivation for reading our book and committing to physical, mental, and spiritual health?
- What do you need to change, adapt, compromise, or reject in order to strengthen your relationship with your body and your body image?

2. Design and create your own **vision board**, illustrating your commitment to love your body.
3. Use **photography** to capture the people, places, and things that inspire you and add pictures to your vision board or FIT Workbook and Gratitude Journal.

Step 1. Gain the Motivation You Need to Change

"Why enter the second half of my life in an aging decrepit vehicle when I could train myself into a younger zippier sports car? While my project was almost entirely physical – run a fast marathon, lose weight, kick the social smoking habit, eat better, get stronger and faster – I also wanted to get happier. I wanted to haul myself out of a midlife malaise and charge into the second act of my life with the wisdom of my years but the piss and vigor of my twenties."

Margaret Webb, 51

Understand the Importance of Motivation

Fitness – mental, physical, emotional, and spiritual – begins with the mind. It starts with your outlook and motivation. What does it take to get motivated and make a commitment to yourself? Optimism and motivation go hand-in-hand. Visualizing a better you and then actually believing you can get there will give you an internal power source that will help you weather the inevitable motivational droughts that lie ahead.

Take our FIT Savvy Quiz™

This quiz will help you see how and why physical activity and a healthy lifestyle are critical for better daily functioning and a happier life. Rev up your mind as you think through your answers to the following questions. (You may already be asking yourself some of them.)

FIT Savvy Quiz

1. **Natural athletic ability is a prerequisite to physical activity.**
   True
   False

2. **Creating a healthy lifestyle doesn't mean you have to make drastic changes all at once.**
   True
   False

3. **Surrounding yourself with people who exercise regularly can help you stick to your fitness program.**
   True
   False

4. **Intrinsic motivation is striving inwardly to be good at something and to reward yourself inwardly for your successes.**
   True
   False

5. **When sticking to a fitness program and beginning to see results, verbal recognition from friends and family, telling you how great you look or asking if you've lost weight, is a form of intrinsic motivation.**
   True
   False

6. **New activities, such as dancing, tai chi, and yoga, engage your brain and challenge it; this is similar to the way physical activity engages your body.**
   True
   False

7. **Adults who spend time each day engaging in physical activity reduce risk factors associated with aging and add years to their lives.**
   True
   False

8. **Exercise doesn't affect your sleep.**
   True
   False

9. **Walking each day can help you build and strengthen muscle mass.**
   True
   False

Answers to our FIT Savvy Quiz

1. **False**
   Natural athletic ability is not a prerequisite to physical activity. Simply focus on the positive changes you are making to your body and mind.

2. **True**
   Drastic changes can be more difficult to stick with. Making small changes in how you live each day can lead to big rewards.

3. **True**
   Studies show that people who take classes with other people, join a team, connect through e-mail, Skype, and online coaching, or work out with other people have the highest fitness success rates.

4. **True**
   When the activity in itself is experienced as rewarding, then there is little need for external motivators. Intrinsic motivation can come from love of a particular activity, self-satisfaction, and a sense of achievement and purpose.

5. **False**
   This is an extrinsic motivator, also known as an outside reward. These types of rewards provide satisfaction and pleasure, but they do not increase the internal motivation as

you try to build your health and fitness program. Extrinsic factors are important to get you started on a new routine. They are great tools for beginners, with intrinsic motivation being the key to determining long-term maintenance of behavior.

6. **True**

Consider your brain a muscle and find ways to engage it, just like your physical body. Keeping your mind active with new experiences and exercise is just as important as working out.

7. **True**

By engaging in daily physical activity, you can reduce your risk of chronic diseases, such as heart disease, high blood pressure, and osteoporosis. You will also experience increased psychological well-being and reduce feelings of depression and anxiety.

8. **False**

Exercise can make your sleep deeper, meaning it will be more refreshing and you will rest more peacefully throughout the night.

9. **True**

However, the building of muscles through walking will depend on the intensity of the walk. It needs to be a brisk walk and include different variations.

Five Strategies for Understanding Motivation

1. Inspiration, Aspiration, Perspiration

Inspiration: People can be a source of inspiration. Seek inspiration from role models and use their stories to help you develop your own.

Aspiration: We all have dreams and goals we want to achieve in our lives. Think about what you aspire to be, experience, or have. Now consider how being healthy and fit will help you get there.

Perspiration: There may be times when the challenge of adhering to a health, fitness, and spirituality program to achieve your new goals becomes overwhelming. There may be times when you hit a few roadblocks along the way. By focusing on progress rather than perfection you can start each day with determination. The key is to never stop trying.

2. Analyze Two Key Factors: Your What and Your Why

What do you want to achieve by creating a healthy lifestyle? Ask yourself:

- Do I believe I can attain my goals?
- Can I picture where I want to be?
- Have I taken the time to plan the path to get there?

You may not be able to control the outcome of all of life's challenges, but you can choose how you evaluate and grow with each experience.

Why is it important that you achieve the goals that you have defined? Take a few minutes and begin to shape your why, since it will fuel your desire, determination, and dedication. You set goals for a reason, so you need to be clear on why you want to achieve specific goals. Your why is what will create your solid foundation. Remember it has to be a strong why; it has to propel you forward and keep you grounded when you feel like giving up.

3. Understand the Importance of Motivation in Starting and Sustaining a Life-Long Health and Fitness Program

As we travel through this journey together, remember that you will be faced with moments when you need to be honest with yourself and clear on why you are doing this. This is how you keep the fire burning; this is how you build momentum.

4. Examine Three Internal "D" Drives: Desire, Determination, and Dedication

Desire: Throughout our book, you will have the opportunity to understand what it is going to take to get you moving and find ways to access the strength and motivation within you just waiting to come alive.

Determination: Once you embrace your desire, it is determination that will carry you to your goals. Focus your mind on what you want. The relentless quest, the energy that keeps you going day after day, will be your determination. If you can stay determined in your quest for your goals, you will succeed.

Dedication: You can define dedication as the price you must pay to achieve what you want. You want to be healthy, to feel good about your body, and you want to be physically and mentally fit. All of this is achievable, but it requires that you commit a certain amount of time to achieve what you want. Real change requires a stick-to-it attitude.

You need dedication to move towards your goals. Keep your resolve strong no matter what obstacles may get in the way. You are capable of achieving your goals. It's not always easy to stay dedicated, but it is imperative if you are to succeed.

On a scale of 1–10, how dedicated are you at this moment to achieving your goals? If your number is not an absolute 10, then you need to go back and revisit your why.

5. Recognize the Differences Between Intrinsic and Extrinsic Motivation

There will be times when you feel tired and are not in the mood to exercise or meditate. When that happens, you are going to need the support of motivators to keep you in the game. Some reasons may be internal and other reasons may be external.

By reflecting on how good you would feel after a workout or meditation, you are activating your intrinsic motivation. That means you are generating positive thoughts about the benefits associated with health, thoughts that can help keep you on track.

But when that isn't enough to keep you in the fitness game, you may need extrinsic motivating rewards. You can buy yourself a new workout outfit that makes you feel great after achieving your goal or you can put away five dollars for each small goal you accomplish and after several months, use the saved money to go on a weekend getaway.

Introducing our FIT Motivational Style Questionnaire™

Understand your unique **FIT Motivational Style** and how it will inspire you to commit to a healthy physical, mental, emotional, and spiritual lifestyle. Once you understand your why and the internal forces that drive you, you are ready to complete our **FIT Motivational Style Questionnaire**, which will help you define the environment that will be most conducive to your health and fitness success.

The **FIT Motivational Style Questionnaire** captures two dimensions that are important for health, fitness, and spiritual success: the social and the competitive. Your **FIT Motivational Style** will be based on the degree to which you are motivated by social participation and competitiveness. For example, the style called "Creative Designer" fits someone who enjoys group participation because it naturally motivates them and provides them with structure. This individual is high in the social dimension, but low in competitiveness.

FIT Motivational Styles should be understood as trends in a person's orientation. The styles are not static but help an individual to get going on the health and fitness process. These styles may evolve as a person's health and fitness increases. You could even move into another style category.

Once you have filled out the **FIT Motivational Style Questionnaire** and calculated your score (see the scoring instructions following the questionnaire), you will discover your **FIT Motivational Style**. This helps to determine the activities and tools that best fit your style and defines the environment that is right for you.

The *FIT Motivational Style Questionnaire*

The following statements involve a variety of situations related to fitness. Read each one carefully and circle the response that best describes what your feelings and attitudes would be if you were in that particular situation.

1. **Today you plan to have a serious workout. You will exercise:**
   1. Alone and at your own pace.
   2. With a friend.
   3. With a team or group.
   4. Following your training plan.

2. **It's Sunday night and you are thinking about your workouts for the week. You:**
   1. Plan what you are going to do ahead of time.
   2. Get to the gym and find out what class you can participate in.
   3. Meet a friend or a group for a morning run or walk.
   4. Go to the gym, get on a treadmill, and push yourself. It's Monday and you want a great start to your week.

3. **You have just moved into your new home and you are excited because of the great park that is nearby. You have been anticipating the invigorating walks you will take in the park each day. As you are leaving for your first walk in the park, a few family members show up. What do you do?**
   1. Pass on going. Say to yourself you'll do it another time when you have no distractions.
   2. Decide there's no rush for the walk. You'll go later that day when time permits.
   3. Tell your family members you were on your way out for a walk and invite them to join you.
   4. As soon as they leave, put on your runners and hit the park with the intention of extending your walk to make up for the slack.

4. **You've just joined a new gym and your plan is to get into better shape. What type of training will you probably go with?**
    1. Ask a personal trainer to give you a program and work with the trainer for a few sessions.
    2. Hit the conditioning area and start pumping some iron. You've done this before so you can figure it out or ask someone there to help.
    3. Check out the class schedule and plan on taking a few classes each week.
    4. Find out if they have any groups that are training, such as running groups, swimming groups, etc.

5. **A 5K walk is being held just blocks away from your house on Sunday. The money raised from the registrations is going to a charitable cause. You decide to:**
    1. Skip it and follow your program at home or at the gym.
    2. Walk over and join in with the spectators to cheer on the walkers.
    3. Call up your friend and ask him or her to join you in the walk.
    4. Sign up and try to challenge yourself by walking the route in the shortest time.

6. **You were planning on working out at the end of the day but are stressed out. You:**
    1. Continue with what needs to get done and plan to work out tomorrow.
    2. Grab a good self-help book, make yourself a cup of tea, and read.
    3. Go to a nearby coffee shop with a friend to chat, and maybe go for a walk together afterwards.
    4. Go for a brisk walk or hit the gym anyway and work the stress out.

7. **You are in a fitness class that you are quite familiar with. Suddenly, the instructor has to leave and asks you to take over the last half of the class. You:**

1. Say you need a little training first, but would like to do it next time. Suggest he or she asks someone else.
2. Agree to take over and try to recall what you have been taught so it's close to the usual class, plus add a few things you think of along the way.
3. Jump in, grab the microphone, and wing it the best you can.
4. Think of this as an opportunity to motivate the group and be seen as a leader.

8. **You arrive at the pool to swim and all of the lanes are busy. You certainly could squeeze your way in, but after evaluating the pool you decide to:**
    1. Check with the lifeguard for the days and times when the pool isn't so busy and plan to return on one of those days.
    2. Go to the conditioning area and work out with weights.
    3. Get in the pool and just do your best to swim with the crowd.
    4. Swim in the lane that looks like it has the more serious swimmers and less splashing.

9. **The yoga class you decide to try turns out to be too advanced for you. You decide to:**
    1. Find another class better suited to your level.
    2. Tell the instructor you are new and need help with the different moves in the class.
    3. Put your mat next to a friendly face or two and try to follow what they are doing.
    4. Challenge yourself and try the moves.

10. **You have been following a training plan to participate in your first 25K charitable bike race. The day of the race you are not feeling your best. You:**
    1. Decide to pass on it and sign up for another race in the near future. This way you can keep your training up to speed.
    2. Put together a care package with a few things you think you may need along the way, e.g. protein bar, aspirin, etc.

3. Go anyway, just taking it easy and staying close to the group of friends you know at the race, letting them know how you're feeling.

4. Tell yourself you'll feel better after the race. You would be more disappointed if you didn't attempt to complete the race.

Calculate Your Score and Analyze the Results

Each time you selected number 1 = 1 point

Each time you selected number 2 = 2 points

Each time you selected number 3 = 3 points

Each time you selected number 4 = 4 points

Add up your total points and read on to discover your **FIT Motivational Style**.

Style 1: Self-Directed Soloist – The Power-from-Within Type

(If you scored 10–17 points)

You prefer to plan out your daily workout schedule. You are self-reliant. Your self-energized style makes it easy for you to go solo when it comes to fitness. You are reasonably comfortable when faced with a sudden change in your planned workout schedule, and your ability to be flexible allows you to make a quick decision on how you will alter your exercise plans. Setbacks are expected. You recognize that you can still achieve your fitness goals. Your strong inner drive keeps you persevering to meet your fitness goals regardless of what gets in the way and how long it takes. Exercises that allow you the opportunity to improve at your own pace suit you best. However, you may enjoy hiring a personal trainer to work with you to map out a detailed plan so when you go it alone there is more structure to your workout.

FIT Activities for the Self-Directed Soloist

Walking, indoor and outdoor cycling, swimming, running, ice skating, in-line skating, gardening, mini-trampoline, home training videos, stair climbing, weight training, yoga

Style 2: Creative Designer – The Light, Energized Type

(If you scored 18–24 points)

An environment that is light and fun motivates you. You like to get inspired by watching others get into action. But you are also the type of person who has the ability to inspire others because of your relaxed, uplifting spirit. You can be playful, yet firm and dedicated in the challenges you take on. You have great energy potential, but the occasional quieting of your mind is essential when your creative juices become exhausted. You have the ability to focus your energy with concentration, combined with enthusiasm and freshness.

When a particular type of exercise turns you on, you can be passionate and hot; but if there is no turn-on, then the energy slows down and things get cold. At that point, you lose interest in the particular activity and need to move on. Your fit is with dance classes, aerobics, or any class that is interesting and has lots of energy to keep your mind activated and your body moving. You may enjoy activities where there is more of a social component and freedom to move around. You don't mind a schedule set out for you when attending a class, but sometimes you might like to hit the gym and just do whatever comes to mind that day.

FIT Activities for the Creative Designer

Walking, indoor and outdoor cycling, dancing, Pilates, running with a partner or group, volleyball, tai chi, weight training, high or low impact aerobic classes, water aerobics

Style 3: Spirited Planner – The Self-Disciplined Social Type

(If you scored 25–31 points)

You are motivated by self-discipline. You like to adhere to structure, but you also enjoy the social component in your activities on occasion. Nature has given you a sophisticated guidance system in your feelings. You have developed an awareness of your emotions, which helps guide you when structuring your daily activities. You also have an adventurous side that comes out in your physical strength, and that is why you are usually open to taking on a new challenge when it comes your way. You may prefer the outdoors so you can participate in a natural environment. You try to remain energetic, lively, and optimistic. You like taking a leadership role and you are good at mastering new skills and teaching others. You like freedom and flexibility because this allows you to have the control to adjust your routine. When you connect passionately to a sport, your inner champion emerges.

FIT Activities for the Spirited Planner

Nature walks, swimming, cross-country skiing, hiking, running, weight training, outdoor and indoor cycling, mountain biking, tennis, tai chi, yoga

Style 4: Competitive Performer – The Play-to-Win Type

(If you scored 32–40 points)

You have a strong achievement orientation. As a competitive performer, you strive hard to reach a goal. You tend to be interested in personal achievement and likely play to win when you take on a challenge. Your practical style represents an independent, determined type. You are ambitious and persistent to be the best you can be, and you have a strong will to always cross the finish line. You are the type who takes training seriously. The thought of performing better than the average keeps your internal flame burning. You train best when you have something to work towards. A competitive goal keeps you focused and motivated.

FIT Activities for the Competitive Performer

Squash, running events, outdoor and indoor cycling, dragon boat racing, golf, martial arts, weight training, specialized dance classes, such as ballroom, salsa, and tango

Note for All FIT Motivational Styles

Review your **FIT Motivational Style** activities. Experiment by sampling activities that fit your own style, as well as ones from the style closest to your score. Be curious and confident as you try out your FIT possibilities. Get ready to develop and nurture a stronger connection with your health and fitness.

Figure 1: Activities for the Four FIT Motivational Styles

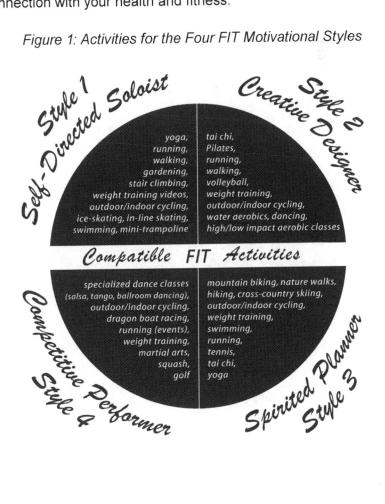

Our Turn…

Susan's Story

My **FIT Motivational Style** is the Creative Designer, with a touch of the Spirited Planner, which perfectly describes my relationship with health and fitness: high energy with lots of body movement and variety in my routines, as well as some quiet time alone for meditation and long walks. I have set up my schedule to provide a lot of variety.

I am motivated by self-discipline. I adhere to structure, but also enjoy social activities on occasion, which I get by working out with other men and women in my condo gym and swimming in the pool. I connect passionately with swimming now, so my inner champion emerges.

I also gave up a car when I moved to downtown Toronto two years ago and take public transit everywhere. This means I often walk one to three hours during the day.

I am open to taking on a new challenge when it comes my way and welcome a quieting of my mind when my creative juices become exhausted. For this reason, I recently took an excellent course in meditation from **The Art of Living Foundation** (Part 3) and have created a habit of doing a daily twenty-minute guided meditation, with a free app from Sri Sri Ravi Shankar, founder of The Art of Living Foundation.

Theresa's Story

My **FIT Motivational Style** in 2010 was the Spirited Planner, with a touch of the Competitive Performer showing up. Today, in 2016, my score shows that I have moved completely into the Competitive Performer.

Throughout the past five years, I have taken on greater challenges physically and that's a result of being involved in the YMCA's yearly fundraisers to get children active and families connected to the YMCA community.

My increased drive to compete is the result of a new belief in what I can achieve. I still enjoy team work and I absolutely love leading my spin classes, but at my core I find that I have a desire to challenge myself and break the mental and physical barriers that I may have been setting for myself earlier.

Your Turn…

Some ideas to get you started:

1. Write in your **FIT Workbook and Gratitude Journal**.
    *   How did you do on the **FIT Savvy Quiz**?
    *   What is your current relationship with your body and with fitness?
    *   What do you want to achieve through health and fitness?
    *   Why is it important to you to achieve the goals that you have defined?
    *   What is your level of motivation at this time?
    *   Can you picture where you want to be?
    *   Have you taken the time to plan the path to get there?
    *   What would help you to find the motivation to achieve that special relationship with health, fitness, and spirituality?
    *   What was your score on the **FIT Lifestyle Questionnaire**?
    *   What areas do you want to improve and what course of action could you take to do this?
    *   What is your **FIT Motivational Style**?
    *   Which activities in your **FIT Motivational Style** do you enjoy most?
    *   Which other activities would you like to try?

2. Illustrate your motivation with images and words and add them to your **vision board**.
3. **Use photography** to capture motivational images and add to your **FIT Workbook and Gratitude Journal**.
4. Turn to Appendix A, Step 1, where you can use tools created by Catherine M. Sabiston and Eva Pila to help you explore your motivation, habits, obstacles, and self-talk, and discover what will help you succeed.

Step 2. Tap Into Your Passion

> *"A lot of curvy people who practice yoga have defined limits in terms of how far they're willing to go. They think they can probably do downward dog or tree pose, but they're not going to try headstands or handstands. They'll say, I'm too fat."*

> *Jessamyn Stanley, 27*

Look Within to Explore Your Passions

We all tend to have our own unique arousal zone that influences the type of activities we like to do. So, look at your health and fitness as a special relationship that is unique to you (and your body), and choose activities that meet your personal desires and needs.

Find Your Unique Connection to Health, Fitness, and Spirituality

Becoming passionate about health, fitness, and spirituality is like finding and developing any good relationship. You must enjoy the activities you participate in and be compatible with the environment you select.

Five Strategies for Developing Your Health, Fitness, and Spiritual Passions

1. Nurture Your Passions

A passion doesn't just happen overnight. It may first take the form of morning walks with a friend, taking the stairs instead of the elevator, or finding some quiet time during the day to meditate. Slowly, over time, you will begin to feel energized and motivated to build a stronger relationship with your body and fitness. As you begin to spend more time participating in new activities, passion will emerge and the desire to make it part of your life will come naturally.

2. *Connect with Your Talents, Strengths, and Interests*

How can you apply your existing talents and gifts to a health and fitness program? Start by viewing these activities as acts of expression and originality. For example, gardening is a talent and a creative outlet, as well as an excellent fitness activity. Other creative passions could be dancing, singing, or writing. Learn new things to challenge your mind and your body. Take courses, do crossword puzzles, learn a new language, or travel!

3. *Think About Sports and Activities You Loved at Other Stages of Life*

Analyze which types of activities you enjoyed the most in the past: individual activities or two-person activities. Did you enjoy bike riding, canoeing, fishing, skating, skiing, or running when you were younger? Did you enjoy jumping rope or playing tennis? Think about whether you enjoyed group activities. Did you like team sports such as baseball, volleyball, curling, soccer, or basketball? Tap into the games and sports you loved doing as a child, such as rolling down a hill, running, rollerblading, bowling, swimming, wrestling, or bike riding. Who did you play with?

4. *Relax Actively: Explore Crafts, Hobbies, and Meditation*

A great way to reduce stress and relax is to take up a creative activity. The act of concentrating and making something with your own hands provides a wonderful sense of satisfaction. Surround yourself with your handmade pieces and celebrate your achievements.

Another way to increase your sense of peace and "being in the moment" is to meditate. It is wonderful way to quiet your mind and feel a sense of gratitude and satisfaction.

5. *View Health and Fitness Activities as Acts of Expression and Originality*

Take time to reflect on yourself and your attributes. Get to know yourself. Write down your thoughts and ideas. You're more likely to keep up with a program that you enjoy. If you love riding your bicycle, consider a spinning class. If you enjoy dancing, an aerobics class that includes dance moves would be a good bet – or a line dancing or Samba class. Plant a vegetable garden and an herb garden and enjoy the rewards of eating fresh produce. Enjoy the act of gardening – planting, weeding, hoeing, raking, mowing, digging, and pruning. Consider any activities that fit your health, budget, and lifestyle. You can evaluate them later.

Our Turn...

Susan's Story

When I joined the YMCA in 2002, I signed up for aerobic fitness classes and reconnected with my passion for dance and music. Today, I still enjoy Zumba classes, both at the gym and on vacation. Over the years, I always appreciated the camaraderie of step classes, weights classes, and low-impact classes. In addition, my husband Peter and I attended a Saturday morning run fit class together. Although I was always at the back of the group, I realized how much I loved moving to the music.

After two years of showing up at the YMCA, I discovered that jogging, walking, and weights had become my passion. From 2004 to 2007 I progressed from the Saturday run fit class to short jogs and long walks. Then I started to compete in races, completing a number of 5K races, 10K races, and half-marathons. In 2004, I won my first medal in a 5K race in Toronto, placing first in my age group.

In 2014, I rediscovered swimming – something I had enjoyed as a child. I created a new medley of strokes for swimming in an outdoor pool and managed to increase the number of laps I swim by committing to the pool three times a week.

Theresa's Story

My fitness passion lies in striving for a big audacious goal. I love to take on a challenge that allows me to access the freedom in believing in myself. Running, of course, is that passion because it is a sport that does not require much, just a pair of running shoes and appropriate clothing based on weather conditions. Running gives me that natural lift and enhances my mood significantly.

My other fitness passion is teaching my spin class. I am always so moved by the energy that can be created when thirty people are all on a mission together on stationary bikes. It is an empowering and, at times, a physically demanding class, but with such great rewards for everyone.

Your Turn...

Some ideas to get you started:

1. Write in your **FIT Workbook and Gratitude Journal** about your passions:
   - What has been your past history with health, fitness, and spirituality?
   - Which sports and activities did you love doing at other stages in your life?
   - Which types of activities did you enjoy the most: individual activities, two-person activities, or team or group activities?
   - Which activities would fit your health, budget, and lifestyle today?
   - How can you apply your existing talents and activities to a fitness program?
   - What new and unique activities would you like to try?
   - How can you nurture your passion for health, fitness, and spirituality?

2. Add images and words to your **vision board** to illustrate your passion.
3. **Use photography** to capture images of your health, fitness, and spiritual passion and add these to your **FIT Workbook and Gratitude Journal**.
4. Turn to Appendix A, Step 2, to discover more tools, created by Catherine M. Sabiston and Eva Pila, to tap into your passions and imagination.

Step 3. Do Your Research

"There is only the striving, the continual striving to find the joy, the thrill, and the love in it."

Margaret Webb, 51

Gain the Knowledge You Need to Move Forward

Part of developing a positive attitude toward health and fitness is doing your own research. What is your current health and fitness level? What are your needs? What types of programs are recommended for women like you, with your needs, limitations, and aspirations?

As you do your research, your knowledge, comfort level, and experience will expand. You will develop a more natural connection to your own health, fitness, and spirituality. Research will help you make informed choices as you plan your new lifestyle. It will be a rewarding process: As you build the foundation of your knowledge, your goals will take shape.

Connect with people, read magazines and books, tap into the Internet, and stay committed to your personal growth and a healthier you. Continue to do research as you improve your health and lifestyle. Find role models in the stories of women who have succeeded before you. This will help your mind to open up to other health and fitness options that are right for you.

Five Strategies for Researching Health, Fitness, and Spirituality

1. *Explore Health and Fitness-Related Retail Outlets, Books, and Magazines*

Visit bookstores and libraries to find success stories, tips, suggestions, and training advice. Find fitness-focused retail outlets that offer training programs for events, as well as equipment, books, and magazines. Talk to the staff and ask questions.

2. *Visit Recreation Centers, Golf Courses, Yoga and Meditation Studios, Community Centers, Gyms and Other Facilities to Learn About Programs*

Search for the best programs and teachers related to your health and fitness passions. The right instructor or trainer can provide you with excellent information and the understanding necessary to enjoy an activity. Sign up for workshops and training sessions offered through retail outlets. Investigate outdoor activity areas in your community, such as nature trails, parks, climbing walls, and hiking paths. Look into other activities, such as water aerobics – an activity you can enjoy for life. Also try out weights classes, yoga classes, and Zumba classes at fitness facilities.

3. *Attend Consumer Shows Related to Women, Health, Lifestyle, Fitness, and Spirituality*

Look at the products and services they display and sell, talk to the exhibitors, read their literature, and visit their websites. Go to free talks and demonstrations by well-known speakers at these shows.

4. *Register for Scheduled Events: Races, Competitions, and Tournaments*

A special event will keep you motivated and committed, and you will have the benefit of learning something new as you train. Research a 5K walk or run, a swim competition, a golf tournament, or a bicycle race to raise money, challenge yourself, and have fun. Form a team for a charity event with a partner, family members, friends, or colleagues. It's a great way to meet your own health and fitness goals, while enjoying time with others.

5. *Look at Websites and Interactive Games and Apps*

Search the Internet for fitness templates, downloads, apps, newsletters, blogs, and videos that are compatible with your **FIT Motivational Style**. Many health, fitness, and consumer websites are convenient ways to expand your knowledge base, get free advice, and find a community of people committed to health and fitness. Surf food-related websites to get recipes for healthy meals and snacks. Sign up for free newsletters or blogs related to health, fitness, and spirituality. Enroll in an online coaching program.

Our Turn...

Susan's Story

When I moved two years ago to a downtown condo, I researched a variety of fitness options nearby – gyms, fitness centers, churches, and parks – and decided for convenience sake to work out early in the morning in my condo gym. I hired a personal trainer to create a new program of weights, bike, and stretching for me.

I also researched apps and videos related to fitness, walking, and weights programs. One of my favorite free apps for guided meditation, which I discovered in my research, is the **Journey Within** from Sattva, featuring Sri Sri Ravi Shankar who is the founder of The Art of Living Foundation (see Part 3).

Theresa's Story

The research I do to gain the knowledge I need to move ahead comes from experts. I train with coaches who know far more than me and inspire me to believe anything is possible. Mark McKoy, Olympic gold medalist and my running coach, teaches me the knowledge I need to become faster and more skilled as a runner so I can work towards my running goal.

Your Turn...

Some ideas to get you started:

1. Write in your **FIT Workbook and Gratitude Journal** about your research.
   - What kinds of research can you do related to fitness, exercise, health, and spirituality?
   - How will this help you along your journey?

- Where can you find free templates, downloads, apps, and videos that are compatible with your **FIT Motivational Style**?
- What do you need to do to develop a healthier relationship with food?
- Which food-related websites can you surf to get tips, ideas, and recipes for healthy meals and snacks?

2. Add to your **vision board**, illustrating your research.
3. **Use photography** to capture people and places that can help with your research.
4. Turn to Appendix A, Step 3, to complete your research activity toolkit, created by Catherine M. Sabiston and Eva Pila.

Step 4. Surround Yourself With Supporters

"If you are losing faith in human nature, go out and watch a marathon."

Kathrine Switzer, 68

Understand the Importance of Building Your Own Support Network

Find the people who believe in you, motivate you, want you to succeed, and check your progress on a regular basis. Studies show that people who take classes with other people, join a team, connect through e-mail and online coaching, or work out with other people have the highest fitness success rates. Surround yourself with people who exercise regularly and practice spirituality. Find someone who will help you to fulfill your own goals and keep your promises. Your dog can become your most important support partner, when walking or jogging!

Five Strategies for Building Your Health, Fitness and Spirituality Community

1. Do Something for Yourself

Make health, fitness, and spirituality top priorities in your life. Schedule workouts and quiet time during the day the way you would arrange an important meeting or appointment. It is a priority on par with work, family, and other commitments. Block off times for physical and mental activity on a regular basis and make sure your friends, family, and colleagues are aware of your commitment. Pay attention to your own needs.

2. Share Your Passion, Goals, and Dreams with Family, Friends, Colleagues, Medical Professionals, Spiritual Leaders, and Health and Fitness Experts

Positive people will be supportive and encouraging in your endeavours. Build trust and honesty into these relationships. Ask, listen, and observe. Share your own knowledge about equipment or exercise ideas with your support network.

Make exercise and fitness a family affair. Ask your partner, spouse, children, and grandchildren to share your activities. Use the weekends to bike, hike, ice skate, play tennis, bowl, golf (or miniature golf), jog, or walk with family and friends. Walk everywhere – in the woods, by the water, in the mall, on a trail, up and down hills, or down the street.

3. Check In on a Regular Basis

Use e-mail, Skype, or phone calls for regular check-ins. Write down your goals, define the terms and check-in times, make them visual, and track your progress. Encourage your support network to offer help and inspiration.

If you work out with someone, you can still go at your own pace. Set your own goals. Your goal could be a half-marathon, your partner's goal a 5K. Register to enter the race to confirm your commitment to the goal.

4. Start a Walking or Running Group

Look for existing walking and running groups on meetup.com and contact the groups directly. Ask your friends, people in your neighborhood, or colleagues at work to join you. Find people with similar goals, such as losing weight, relieving stress, enjoying nature, finding a jogging routine, or hiking. Decide when, where, and how often you will walk or run and whether you will walk outdoors or indoors. Map out your routes and continue to add distance and increase the level of difficulty. Prepare the right equipment for walking or running: a pedometer (your goal should be 10,000 steps each day), an appropriate type of shoe, identification, a water bottle, cash, a cell phone, and a map. After each walk or run with your group, gather for a healthy breakfast, lunch, or latte at a local restaurant or cafe.

Monitor your progress in your **Weekly FIT Training Log** (the distance you walked, how long it took, the difficulty of your route, your level of enjoyment, and your thoughts and challenges).

5. *Hire a Personal Trainer, Coach, or Mentor*

Look for a certified expert to provide a personalized assessment and develop a realistic plan to achieve your fitness and health goals. If possible, get a referral. An experienced trainer can sense the need for minor or major changes in the frequency, intensity, and duration of your fitness program. He or she can provide a stronger foundation by teaching you proper exercise form. To cut costs, share personal training sessions with your partner, friends, or colleagues.

Some things to consider when selecting and working with a personal trainer: What is the personality of the trainer? Does he or she listen to you, explain everything clearly, feel passionate about their work, motivate you, and have a sense of humor? Ask for a resume or biography and evaluate the person's education in exercise science or medicine, certification from an accredited organization, up-to-date knowledge and skills, experience with people your age, and experience with people with medical conditions.

Our Turn...

Susan's Story

As a child, I was short, overweight, and self-conscious, and I was always the last person picked for sports teams. That is when I developed my preference for individual sports and classes, which have been part of my life since then. Over the years, I have been lucky to enjoy a strong support system for fitness and spirituality, including my family, friends, and colleagues.

I have taken many fitness classes throughout my life and was always motivated by the women and men in these classes, as well as by the teachers. In 2005, one of my closest friends and fellow gym members, Pat McMonagle, said she would go out with me once a week to help me to prepare for my first full marathon. In the end, Pat joined me at both marathons I completed and talked me through the last 10 km to the finish line. Both of my daughters also joined me in these races and cheered me on. In addition, my husband, Peter, met me at 37 km and joined Pat to bring me in at both of the marathons.

Theresa's Story

The ways I continue to build my health and fitness community are by getting to my YMCA at least four times a week, teaching my amazing group of spinning participants and friends and eating the foods that I know are healthy and make me feel good. Now a delicious treat – occasionally, like ice cream – can feel good too and I believe that once in a while it's a great way to reward yourself and have some fun.

Your Turn...

Some ideas to get you started:

1. Write in your **FIT Workbook and Gratitude Journal** about your support network.
    - Who will you include in your health, fitness, and spirituality network?
        - Partner or spouse
        - Children
        - Grandchildren
        - Friends
        - Colleagues
        - Team or league
        - Mentors and coaches
        - Certified trainer
        - Your dog
    - What steps have you taken, or plan to take, to build your team?
    - Who can you ask to support your fitness commitments and hold you accountable?
    - Make a fitness pact and decide who will be included.
    - Which of the following strategies can you adapt?
        - Make exercise and fitness a family affair.

- Start a walking or running group.
- Sign up for a team sport or a league.
- Join a curling club, a hiking club, a cycling group, or a running group.
- Join an online community.
- Find a fitness meetup to join.
- Hire a personal trainer, coach, or mentor (offline or online) to get you started and to keep you on track.
- Register for an online course or program.

2. Illustrate your support community on your own **vision board**.
3. **Use photography** to capture your health, fitness, and spirituality community.
4. Turn to Appendix A, Step 4, to take Catherine M. Sabiston and Eva Pila's survey on support networks and make a plan to build your community of supporters.

Step 5. Believe You Can Achieve Your Goals

"I am proof that it's possible. I'm also proof that there's no end goal to this challenge. Though we can achieve goals along the way, we can't ever achieve super fitness then set it on the mantle like some trophy collecting dust. Super fitness entails a continual striving to improve wellness, in every way."

Margaret Webb, 51

Analyze the Role of Goal Setting

The first step towards having unstoppable motivation, a key element of mental and physical fitness, is to determine your goals. Smaller goals that lead to a bigger goal are less overwhelming. They therefore improve your success rate.

Studies have shown that people who set clear decisive goals are more likely to achieve what they have set out to do and as a result have a higher success rate. If you set out to start exercising or meditating without specific goals, chances are you will find yourself directionless at times and at a greater risk of giving up.

Every day, visualize each of your goals as complete. Visualization is one of the most important ingredients to success.

Unless you write down and track your goals, they are likely to get lost in the shuffle and excitement of new problems, new challenges, and new decisions. Chart your progress and make adjustments to your goals and plan.

Understand Your FIT Motivators™

Each **FIT Motivation Style** has corresponding **FIT Motivators**, based on what will work best for you. Understanding your **FIT Motivators** will help you achieve success in setting and achieving your goals.

FIT Motivators for the Self-Directed Soloist

Keep a journal of what you are doing or, even better, put up a cork or vinyl board and track your workouts so you can see how you are doing whenever you pass by the board. Reward yourself for sticking to your program.

FIT Motivators for the Creative Designer

Displaying a visual that maps out how you are doing with your goals can be quite a motivator. Use cork or Bristol board for this project. Design a one-month calendar to document your workouts. Make it attractive by cutting out colorful, uplifting pictures of health and fitness from different magazines. Paste or tape them onto your board to add a little pizazz to your calendar. Now hang it up so you see it each day and start to track your progress. Make sure you have some colorful markers nearby for marking your daily workouts. This will be a way to energize that creative designer within you and inspire you to keep moving toward your goals.

FIT Motivators for the Spirited Planner

Nothing is more motivating to you than measurable results – results you can feel both physically and emotionally on your quest to optimal health and fitness. Your love of nature makes the outdoors a great place to do some of your best thinking. Keep a **Weekly FIT Journal** listing your goals and how you are doing. Add notes to this journal about what you learn throughout your journey in health and fitness, about yourself and others. This is a good way to feed your mind. It will provide you with new information as you master your workouts. The journal can become a great resource for you to share your experiences with others, who may be looking for pointers on how to stay motivated in their health and fitness.

FIT Motivators for the Competitive Performer

Register for an upcoming sporting event in your community to keep your competitive spirit energized. Signing-up and planning your training program for the event will get that high-performance adrenalin flowing. Your love of knowledge regarding self-improvement can be nurtured by picking up an informative training book. Begin to track your training days in your **Weekly FIT Training Log**, adding a few notes about how you are feeling, the food you have been eating, and tidbits about what you have learned as you train for the event. Evaluating your progress at the end of a week is a great way for you to keep motivated. Look for ways to optimize your program.

Five Strategies for Defining Success and Setting Goals

1. *Include a Variety of Goals*

- Mental health goals
- Cardio goals
- Strength goals
- Flexibility goals
- Balance goals
- Food and nutrition goals

2. *Set SMART Goals*

- **Specific**: Your goals must be very specific.
- **Measurable**: You can measure your successes.
- **Achievable**: For example, complete a 5K race or stick to your twice a week yoga class for a month.
- **Realistic**: Choose what's right for your body and current health status.
- **Time-related**: With specific dates in your **FIT Action Plan**, set a real timeframe in which to accomplish these goals.

3. Set Smaller and Bigger Goals

Keep an eye on the distant goal and you will steadily improve and achieve it. Another important point to consider when defining your goals is to take your big goals and break them down into smaller, easy to achieve, short-term goals. Smaller goals that lead to a bigger goal are less overwhelming. They therefore improve your success rate.

For example, if your long-term goal is to run in a 10K charitable event at the end of the summer, then you can break down that challenge into two training stages. Stage one is to train towards running five kilometers within one month. Stage two is to run the ten kilometers by the end of the second month. This is a strategy that sets you up for success.

Or you could start with goals for twelve weeks. For three months commit to an activity from your **FIT Motivational Style**. Then, reassess it. The idea is to set good goals: ones that are important to you, tell you where you are going, and show how far you have to go. The secret is to align your goals with your basic values.

4. Identify Obstacles, Strategies to Overcome Them, and Rewards

Short-term goals give you milestones for staying sharp and motivated throughout the journey. They also help you to deal with setbacks and fluctuations. Make small changes on a daily basis to create the steppingstones towards positive habits. Maintain a positive mental attitude. Find ways to celebrate when you achieve a goal and watch your enthusiasm increase and your confidence soar.

5. Be Energized by the Progress You Make

Be patient with yourself. It may take time to see the results, but as time progresses, you will be advancing towards your goals. Aim high and focus your energy, reduce distractions, and find new ways to achieve your goals.

The process of sitting down and mapping out your goals is a powerful technique. You will be designing a plan that provides you with direction. This will help you to stay focused. It's important to have a vision of what you want to achieve. It's okay to dream about how you want to feel and look physically, but to actualize those dreams you need specific and realistic goals.

Our Turn...

Susan's Story

Because I am a Creative Designer, I know how important it is for me to have an environment that is light and fun. I want to be around other people who inspire me and support me in my efforts. I also enjoy watching other people in their health and fitness pursuits: lifting weights, running, swimming, or walking, and I take the time to encourage and congratulate them.

Once I rediscovered swimming laps, I wanted to continue to swim throughout the winter. However, I realized that if I joined a club to swim early in the morning in the winter, I would not sustain my fitness goals. To get up very early in the morning, take the subway in winter weather, swim, and come home would be difficult for me to maintain. So I have chosen to build my cardio workouts on an indoor bike in my gym and continue to swim in the summer. Above all, I do not want to sabotage the health and fitness goals and habits that I have worked so hard to create and sustain.

My long-term goals are to continue to do weight and strength training, to walk everywhere, to keep my body healthy and uninjured, and to retain my mobility.

Theresa's Story

The best way I get motivated is by setting goals, something to reach for in the future. I find that a goal helps create structure for me and it gives direction. When I have a clear picture of what I am aiming for, I know what is expected of me and what I need to do to reach my goal.

Your Turn...

Some ideas to get you started:

1. Write in your **FIT Workbook and Gratitude Journal** about your goals:
    *   Define success for your health and fitness.
    *   What goals have you already accomplished in your life?
    *   What are your goals for health and fitness?
        -   Body goals
        -   Cardio goals
        -   Strength goals
        -   Flexibility and balance goals
        -   Food and nutrition goals
        -   Mindfulness goals
    *   What is your biggest goal, with a completion date?
    *   What are your short-term goals?
    *   What are your blue-sky goals?
    *   Set goals for specific times:
        -   Your immediate goals
        -   One-week goals
        -   One-month goals
        -   Six-month goals
        -   One-year goals
        -   Five-year goals
        -   Ten-year goals
2. Illustrate your goals on your own **vision board**.
3. **Use photography** to capture images that represent your goals and add them to your **FIT Workbook and Gratitude Journal**.
4. Turn to Appendix A, Step 5, for Catherine M. Sabiston and Eva Pila's research, tools and activities on setting goals.

PART 2

EMBRACE YOUR LIFE

Step 6. Develop Habits and Routines Aligned with Your Goals

"I can report that training has become a happy habit. I actually look forward to runs, pumping weight, doing yoga, and moving my body in a myriad of ways."

Margaret Webb, 51

Creating lifetime health, fitness, and spirituality habits can seem like an impossible task, requiring significant time and effort. The thought of fitting something else into an already crowded life seems impossible to many. However, the habits you develop determine your health. The simple things you do on a daily basis can lead to disease or to a sense of well-being and longevity.

Most people have started a health, fitness, and spirituality program more than once. It may be hard for you to stick to your program for a variety of reasons: you lose the energy and enthusiasm, other things distract you, or you don't see results quickly enough.

Understand the most effective ways to break old habits, stay focused, and develop new routines. Fitness and health are a way of life that involves patience, persistence, and maintaining good habits. Your goal is to simplify your life and find ways to sustain your habits, through periods of high and low motivation.

Five Strategies for Maintaining New Habits and Routines

1. *Examine Your Health, Fitness, and Spirituality Routines that Work Now*

Research shows that the best way to establish a new habit is to attach it to an existing habit or commitment. Which routines do you do on a weekly basis that connect to your health, fitness, and spirituality?

- Morning routines
- Lunchtime routines

- Evening routines
- Weekly routines
- Weekend routines
- Work routines
- Family routines
- Travel routines

2. *Analyze the Habits and Routines that Interfere with Your Goals*

What would you gain by changing your habits? Think about what would motivate you to reduce, give up, or eliminate the habits that get in your way in order to achieve your goals. What can you substitute for your unwanted thoughts, feelings, or behaviors?

3. *Develop Strategies for Embracing New Habits and Routines*

List the benefits of new habits and routines. Make your goals public: share them with everyone!

4. *Create Daily Rituals to Help You Sustain Positive Habits and Routines*

Simplify your life with some – or all – of these daily habits.

- Smile
- Eat breakfast
- Hydrate
- Take a few deep breaths
- Pack your gym bag
- Pack healthy snacks
- Stretch for ten minutes
- Listen to music
- Say a positive affirmation
- Go for a walk or jog
- Take the stairs
- Meditate
- Practice yoga

5. *Set Up Online and Off-line Systems to Monitor Your Habits and Routines*

When you track and monitor your habits and routines, you can assess the results:

*   You are getting a good night's sleep.
*   You think more clearly.
*   You have more energy.
*   You can lift heavier weights.
*   You can work out longer without feeling exhausted.
*   You notice your resting heart rate drop over time.
*   You hear your doctor congratulate you on your improved health.
*   Your clothes fit better.

Our Turn...

Susan's Story

As an entrepreneur and an independent spirit, I spent my life resisting habits and routines. Now, over the past two years, I have learned to embrace them and experience the benefits of an organized, low-stress life. For these reasons, I try to get up, go to the gym to work out, meditate, and eat breakfast at about the same time every day. In order to commit to this morning schedule, I changed my sleeping habits.

Since I work out of a home office, I try to spend a maximum of an hour at a time in front of the computer, and then move around. I take breaks from work throughout the day, to get outside, to eat a meal, to read a book, to shop, or to talk to friends and family. The one old habit I have to avoid is wandering into the kitchen to snack on crackers during the day, since I am usually not really hungry.

About five years ago, I started to consciously think about eating simply and sensibly and to cut out mindless snacking. For this reason, I always keep nuts, apples, and oranges as snacks in my purse and at my desk. I drink lots of water. And I still indulge in small portions of the things I enjoy, such as chocolates and ice cream.

Theresa' s Story

I'm a morning person so I find getting up early and having my gym bag packed the night before and waiting at the door makes it easier to head out to the Y at 6:30 am. Hitting the gym in the morning is a great way to start my day. This time prepares me for the rest of the day and sets me up powerfully and stress free.

Your Turn...

Some ideas to get you started:

1. Write in your **FIT Workbook and Gratitude Journal** about your old and new habits and routines.
    - What habits do you currently have that interfere with your goals?
        - Eating habits
        - Sleeping habits
        - Work habits
        - Smoking
        - Drinking habits
        - Other
    - What would motivate you to give up, reduce, or eliminate those habits in order to achieve your health and fitness goals? What can you substitute for your unwanted thoughts, feelings, or behaviors?
    - What fitness routines do you currently have that work and you want to maintain?
        - Morning routines
        - Lunchtime routines
        - Evening routines
        - Weekly routines
        - Weekend routines
    - What new routines do you want to create?
    - What kind of tracking systems will help you to monitor your habits and routines?
    - What changes can you start with?

2. Illustrate your new habits and routines on your own **vision board**.

3. **Use photography** to capture images of your habits and routines.

4. Turn to Appendix A, Step 6, by Catherine M. Sabiston and Eva Pila, to find out how your mood and emotion regulation can affect your ability to change habits and keep new routines.

Step 7. Create Your Own Action Plan

"Life is for participating, not for spectating."

Kathrine Switzer, 68

Develop Realistic Health, Fitness, Nutrition, and Spirituality Plans

Unrealistic plans for fitness and health can be a recipe for failure, quickly turning your optimism and positive vision into a sea of doubt and despair.

Ensure your plan includes time for the ups and downs of your life. Make allowances for vacations, parties, and other breaks. Foster self-compassion during times when you are not able to adhere to your original goals. Emotional health is extremely important and directly impacts physical health.

Remember that workout plans are simply estimates. When you are not able to stick to your schedule, make a mental plan for the next time you will tackle your goal. Flexibility and compassion towards yourself during times of challenge will directly impact your motivation and goal attainment in the future.

Convert Your Goals and Habits into a Customized FIT Action Plan™

Try to incorporate suggested activities from your **FIT Motivational Style** into your program, for on-going success.

Style 1: Self-Directed Soloist

Walking, indoor and outdoor cycling, swimming, running, ice-skating, in-line skating, gardening, mini-trampoline, home training videos, stair climbing, weight training, and yoga.

Style 2: Creative Designer

Walking, indoor and outdoor cycling, dancing, Pilates, running (with a partner or group), volleyball, tai chi, weight training, high or low impact aerobic classes, and water aerobics.

Style 3: Spirited Planner

Nature walks, swimming, cross-country skiing, hiking, running, weight training, indoor and outdoor cycling, mountain biking, tennis, tai chi, and yoga.

Style 4: Competitive Performer

Squash, running events, indoor and outdoor cycling, dragon boat racing, golf, martial arts, weight training, and specialized dance classes, such as ballroom, salsa, and tango.

Five Strategies for Embracing Your Health and Fitness Plan

1. *Find New Ways to Incorporate Mental, Physical, Spiritual, and Nutritional Activities into Your Daily Life*

Morning

- Stretch every morning, to ease back pain, improve your posture and joint health, prevent injury, diminish stress, strengthen your muscles, increase your flexibility, and enhance your sleep.
- Find time to meditate and be present each day. Set aside ten to twenty minutes and you will notice how it increases your energy levels, happiness, and inner peace throughout the day. Breathe in and out and be aware of your breath.
- Take a shower in the morning.
- Before you jump into the shower, do a few sets of push-ups, crunches, and squats. Morning exercise elevates your metabolism.
- Eat a healthy breakfast.

- Fit a few stretches or sit-ups in while waiting for your morning coffee to brew.
- Hop onto the treadmill or stationary bicycle while you listen to the radio, watch the morning news, or relax with your iPod.
- Step outside for a brisk walk.
- Allow yourself enough time to eat something light before you hit the gym or start to exercise. Exercising on an empty stomach will cause your body to break down muscle in order to have enough energy. Once you've adjusted to early-morning workouts, add to the routine.
- Play some golf before heading off to work.
- Swim early in the morning, when pools are not as busy.
- Drink warm water with lemon as a soothing and enjoyable beverage to accompany breakfast in the morning.

Lunchtime

- Whether you eat lunch at home or at work, take a break and devote this time to you.
- Join a gym and attend a noon-hour class. Shower and enjoy the second half of your day.

Evenings

- A great opportunity for some quick calisthenics. Do some basic exercises for ten to twenty minutes – jumping jacks, stretches, jogging on the spot, jumping rope, sit-ups, and crunches. Consider lifting light dumbbells or doing arm circles, squats, lunges, and push-ups during television commercials.
- If you are a night owl, try not to exercise too late. Working out too close to bedtime, such as an hour before you go to sleep, will disrupt your sleep.

Throughout the day

- Ride a bicycle to and from work, on errands, or along trails.
- Get on and off the subway, streetcar, or bus several stops before your destination and walk to work, or park at the farthest end of a parking lot.

- Do errands on foot instead of by car.
- Take hills instead of going around them.
- Squeeze in a few ten-minute walks throughout the day. If you don't have time for a full workout, recognize the value of shorter spurts of exercise spaced throughout the day.

At Work

- Leave a comfortable pair of walking shoes at work. Go for a short walk with colleagues or drive to a nearby mall and walk. Take walking breaks throughout the day.
- Put a pair of hand-grippers in your drawer. These provide a great finger and forearm workout and can be done while on long conference calls or between e-mails.
- If your commute involves riding the bus or train or you drive and often have to sit in stalled traffic, take along and use a pair of hand-grippers.

After Work

- Go to the gym on your way home.
- Take a walk before or after dinner.

On Weekends

- Any sort of incremental physical activity adds up and can greatly benefit your health and well-being.
- Rethink your weekend rituals. Try a Saturday bike ride, a rock-climbing lesson, or a swim in a pool.
- Look for scenic routes for weekly walks and bike rides with your family, friends, or alone all year round.

2. *Create Specific Action Plans, for the Gym and at Home*

Gym Action Plan

Some women don't join a gym because they feel self-conscious about their bodies, don't understand how to use machines, and feel they don't fit into the gym culture. They visit once and never return. This is one of the most commonly cited reasons that women disengage and drop out of physical activity. The gym is a naturally evaluative environment and places a huge focus on the body.

Three effective strategies to reduce self-consciousness at the gym are to increase mindfulness, to turn inward and focus on the self, and to practice self-compassion. Also:

- Get an orientation tour of the gym and ask staff to explain the machines.
- Tell the teacher of the class you attend that you are new. You will receive extra support from the teacher and from other participants.
- Go to the gym with someone who is experienced, such as a friend or colleague.
- Ask staff members your questions and seek advice.
- Hire a personal trainer. Find out if they offer group training, which is more affordable.
- Attend a yoga class. The expectations of others can push you to succeed.
- Offer friendly support when you see someone struggling to understand a machine or a class.

Home Action Plan

Exercising at the gym is certainly not best for everyone. Research shows that any type of bodily movement is beneficial; it does not have to be a structured exercise program at the gym. Physical and spiritual activities at home are equally helpful if that is a more conducive environment for you.

Create a sanctuary at home: a place devoted to you, which is quiet and stress-free. Fill it with:

- A mat
- A cushion
- Candles
- Essential oils
- Your **FIT Workbook and Gratitude Journal**
- Music

Try different types of meditation, such as walking meditations and seated meditations, to find the one you enjoy the most.

3. *Design Vacation and Business Trip Action Plans*

Vacation Action Plan

Well-documented research shows that having a contingency plan regarding exercise and nutrition for vacations and trips is the most effective way to maintain your goals. Ultimately, flexibility is more important than rigidity. If you are unable to maintain your scheduled physical activities or plans, engaging in travel-related physical activities is a great alterative! You might consider hiking, playing on the beach, snorkeling, scuba diving, bicycle rentals, and walking. Contact tourism associations to find parks and walking and hiking routes throughout your trip.

Also, adjust your goals to be more general. For example, "During my vacation, I will try to engage in at least one thing that is physically active and I will try at least one new activity during my trip." Here are other easy, inexpensive suggestions:

- Walk in deep water.
- Play beach volleyball.
- Build sand castles with children and grandchildren.
- Take long walks in the sand.

Business Trip Action Plan

- When you go on a business trip, check online for fitness facilities where you'll be staying.
- When booking your hotel, find out what fitness facilities they have, such as a pool and gym.
- Bring along your exercise clothes and equipment, including resistance bands, a bathing suit, shorts, T-shirts, and workout shoes.
- When you arrive, ask for walking and jogging maps and routes near the hotel.

4. *Develop Your Own Online FIT Action Plan*

Develop an online or mobile plan to track and complement your **Weekly FIT Training Log**, using Fitbit or phone tracker. Use a physical activity tracking device to better monitor your progress. Pedometers are inexpensive and easy to use tools to track your activity. Researchers recommend aiming for 10,000 steps per day to achieve maximum health benefits.

5. *Kick-Start Your Health and Fitness Program with a* **Weekly FIT Training Log™**

After each workout, track your progress in your **Weekly FIT Training Log**, and use the same template to plan next week's acitivites:

My *Weekly FIT Training Log*

Week of _____

My fitness goal for the week is

_____

Promise to Self

I promise to _____

What are my needs in order to achieve my goal for the week? For example, one hour for me between 6 a.m. and 7 a.m. Be specific:

My Partners

    1.

    2.

    3.

My Training Schedule
(include times)
Sunday:
Monday:
Tuesday:
Wednesday:
Thursday:
Friday:
Saturday:

My Body Log
(aches and pains)

My Food Log

My Mood Log
(reflections and comments)

What was my overall attitude and mood this week?

What were my challenges?

How can I improve my training approach for next week?

Our Turn...

Susan's Story

My **FIT Action Plan** on weekdays involves three days of weight training and two days of swimming or stationary biking. I have a variety of weights exercises in my program. To keep from becoming bored, I vary each workout session.

On weekends, I walk for hours to explore a neighbourhood, attend an event, or to try a new restaurant, instead of taking the car or public transport. Having a destination in mind before I go helps me to relax and appreciate the scenery along the way.

On vacations, I check out the hotel fitness facility and pool when I arrive at a new destination. I ask at the desk whether they have walking or jogging trails mapped out. When I am on a cruise, I find out which free classes are offered on the ship, such as Zumba and stretch, and try to take advantage of them.

Theresa' s Story

I love the early mornings when it comes to doing my work out. I head to the Y around 6:30 a.m. This time is perfect for me to do my weight training because it is quiet and the space is not very crowded. I enjoy moving through my weight routine with ease.

My **FIT Action Plan** consists of teaching two spin classes a week, running two to three times per week, and weight training three to four times per week. I find when I circuit train with weights it's exactly like the cardio days. I know that it doesn't matter what I am doing, cardio training always sneaks in – it's all about getting your heart rate up.

I am fortunate to be training with my amazing Olympic gold coach, Mark McKoy. We hit the hills for a run because it is the best place to get faster and that's exactly what I am aiming for. Also on Saturdays after the run I teach an indoor cycling class to a great group of thirty people at the Y.

On vacation, I usually look for accommodations with an indoor gym I can use. But usually my workouts consist of walking and tons of relaxation. I believe the body needs time to rejuvenate and for me that means being okay with a lighter routine while on holidays.

Your Turn…

Some ideas to get you started:

1. Write in your **FIT Workbook and Gratitude Journal** about your **FIT Action Plan**.
   - How can you incorporate fitness into your daily life?
   - What are the best times?
   - What are the best places?
   - What are the best activities for you?
   - Describe your **FIT Action Plan** for one week.
   - Describe your online strategy and plan.
   - What can you include in your program for special times:
     - Holidays
     - Business trips
     - Family Trips
     - Vacations
2. Illustrate your **FIT Action Plan** on your own **vision board**.
3. **Use photography** to capture images for your **FIT Action Plan**.
4. Turn to Appendix A, Step 7, to find worksheets, a tracking tool, and graph designed by Catherine M. Sabiston and Eva Pila to help you with your **FIT Action Plan**.

Step 8. Acknowledge Challenges and Stay Motivated

"Your body is not standing in your way. Only your mind is standing in your way."

Jessamyn Stanley, 27

Recognize and Face Your Challenges

If you're like most of us, you resist change. Stress, excitement, doubt, and fear are emotions you may feel when you start – and as you're sustaining – a health, fitness, and spirituality program. You don't always know what obstacles or setbacks are coming or even recognize them when they occur. Work projects, family commitments, and social lives – all these things can derail your commitment.

Find Ways to Overcome Challenges and Recommit to Yourself

Don't listen to your negative inner voice, the one that doesn't want discomfort or inconvenience. It will deplete the power source within you. View setbacks as learning experiences: assess your feelings, understand the problems and obstacles, and find different ways to reconnect. Embrace the changes. Persistence is the key. Find the incentives you need to motivate you. Realize that you are tougher on yourself than you are on others. Take a look back and see how you got to where you are today. Chances are you'll see a path of persistence, perseverance, and progress. Look for continuous improvement over time.

Understand your FIT Detractors™ based on Your FIT Motivational Style

Style 1: Self-Directed Soloist

Because you are self-motivated and stick to your own agenda, you probably like routine and habituate pretty quickly once you find something that works. You could run into the rigidity zone, so make it a point to review your plan at least once a month to see how you might tweak it and add some new zest. Continue to challenge yourself with new activities.

Style 2: Creative Designer

Because you are light in nature and your environment can have a major influence on the way you feel and on your health and fitness, stay away from environments that generate low energy. Connect with people and spaces that add to your enthusiasm, and with people who have a similar uplifting spirit. This will help you succeed in your health and fitness pursuits.

Style 3: Spirited Planner

Be sure to balance your personal health and fitness time with the responsibilities you tend to take on. It is important for you to stay connected with your inner self and stay consistent in your routine. Your natural love of connecting with people is a positive strength. Just be sure to devote equal time to yourself. These private moments will prove to be rejuvenating: a good way to stay systematic and structured in your plan.

Style 4: Competitive Performer

The driver within you needs to keep moving, so be sure to keep those competitive goals always in the forefront. Seek environments that nurture self-improvement. Also be cognizant of your need for recovery periods and don't overdo your training. Too much of a good thing can lead to injury and burnout. Be sure to nurture your inner competitive performer and reward yourself for your hard work.

Five Strategies to Overcome Challenges and Refocus

1. *Recognize and Acknowledge Challenges that Interfere with Your Progress*

Concentrate on the whole experience, both the good and the bad. Stay focused on the solution, not on the problem.

- Sometimes challenges involve **physical** problems, such as injury and illness.
- For some people, the obstacles are **emotional,** such as depression, hormone imbalances, sleep apnea, food allergies, unhealthy relationships, perfectionism, or addiction.
- They can also be **time-related**: too busy with work or family responsibilities.
- Sometimes they are **money-related**: you can't afford to continue at a gym.
- **Family-related**: care-giving responsibilities, family illness, or the death of a loved one can stand in the way of you and your goals.

2. *Find Ways to Accept Challenges and Refocus with Support Strategies and Tools*

Be fully present in your life. Find the incentives you need to motivate you. Realize that you are tougher on yourself than you are on others. Take a look back and see how you got to where you are today. Chances are you'll see a path of persistence, perseverance, and progress. Look for continuous improvement over time.

3. *Use Inspirational Quotes and Strong Statements to Stay Motivated*

Strong statements increase your belief, confidence, and motivation. Think about these on a daily basis and analyze what they mean to you. Create desktop wallpaper with quotes and sayings you love and post quotes on your vision board, bathroom mirror, or wall. They will give you the visual inspiration you need to overcome obstacles and stay motivated.

4. Revise Your Self-Talk and Use Daily Affirmations

Affirmations are proven methods of self-improvement because of their ability to rewire your brain.

5. Use Positive Thinking to Re-Energize and Inspire You Through Setbacks

- First thing in the morning, pause and bless the day. Take a few deep breaths. Add breaks throughout your day to reconnect with your spiritual essence and to express gratitude.
- Set aside time for yourself. The more you build silent moments into your life, the more you'll be able to experience a quiet state of mind anywhere, even in the midst of chaos.
- Plan quiet time for yourself each day and meditate. Find a place inside yourself where you can be totally peaceful in order to enhance your total health.
- Listen to relaxation CDs, such as Tibetan chants and Buddhist meditations.
- Take a silent lunch – no cell phones, text messaging, or reading.
- Stop and smell the roses – literally.
- The feeling that comes from believing that you're enhancing your life will make it easier to recommit.

Our Turn...

Susan's Story

My environment has a major influence on how I feel about fitness and meditation. If I visit the gym in my complex and it is too crowded, I find it difficult to exercise. I try to find times early in the morning when the gym is quiet and I can work out without too many distractions. Noise, music, too much light, and too many people challenge me when I am trying to focus on my body.

Although I have completed a variety of races over the past ten years, I recently decided to limit my races to one 10K and one half-marathon per year. This is enough to keep me motivated without adding stress. I also attend races as a spectator, to cheer on both friends and strangers.

When I am on vacation, I often find it hard to maintain my healthy eating and fitness routines. At these times, I encourage myself to enjoy the vacation, do what I can, and return to my routines when I get back home.

Theresa's Story

Fitness is my priority in life. It activates every cell in my body and gives me a zest for living well. I am a much better person for me and for others when I am active and feeling healthy.

The only issue I have related to my health is my skin condition, vitiligo. During the summer months I find it a challenge to go outdoors to exercise because of my sensitivity to the sun and the potential destruction of my pigmentation. If I am going to go for a run in the summer, I have to start before 7 a.m. to avoid the warmer, more intense hours of sun. But I always find a way and usually it's by staying inside. It always works.

Your Turn...

Some ideas to get you started:

1. Write in your **FIT Workbook and Gratitude Journal**.
    - Describe the ways in which you have responded to changes in you life.
    - What have been your health and fitness obstacles or setbacks in the past?
      - Money-related
      - Physical problems, such as injury or illness
      - Time-related
      - Emotional obstacles
      - Family-related
    - What are your challenges, based on your **FIT Motivational Style**?
    - What might interfere with your progress in the future?
    - What can you do when that happens?

- How can you use positive thinking to re-energize and inspire you through setbacks?
- What incentives do you need to motivate yourself?
- How can you add mindfulness to your life every day?

2. Add to your own **vision board**, illustrating your challenges and ways to refocus.

3. **Use photography** to capture images of your challenges and ways to refocus.

4. Turn to Appendix A, Step 8, to find tools designed by Catherine M. Sabiston and Eva Pila to help you meet challenges and use self-compassion to stay motivated.

Step 9. Recognize and Celebrate Your Achievements

"When I go to the Boston Marathon now, I have wet shoulders – women who fall into my arms crying. They're weeping for joy because running has changed their lives. They feel they can do anything."

Kathrine Switzer, 68

Understand the Importance of Rewards to Sustain a Healthy Lifestyle

Everyone needs encouragement, and rewards are one of the best incentives to keep you motivated. Think of the bonus systems that spark employees to reach extraordinary sales goals. Why should it be any different for you and your health and fitness? You will be more successful in your journey if you find ways to reward yourself. You deserve it.

Celebrate Short- and Long-Term Achievements

To stay motivated, you need to recognize your progress, not merely track it. The key is to find different ways to reinforce your health and fitness successes. These can range from complimenting yourself on your efforts to making a pact with a partner to celebrate milestones along the way. The act of reinforcement itself is more important than the method.

Five Strategies for Designing Rewards and Celebrating Success

1. *Reward Yourself for Behavioral Changes, as well as Strength-Based Changes*

Success includes breaking old habits and creating new routines. The more you reward yourself for progress, the more motivated you will feel about reaching new milestones and, finally, accomplishing your goals.

2. Acknowledge Small Daily Successes

Look in the mirror every day, smile, and say "I love you," or "You're doing great!" Then say, "Thank you," smile, and go on with your day.

3. Develop Strategies to Celebrate Being Faithful to Your New Routines

Here are some suggestions for ways to celebrate your new routines:

- Browse a bookstore or library
- Write yourself a love letter on what you appreciate in yourself
- Meditate
- Go to your favourite restaurant alone, order your favourite meal, relax, and read a book
- Give thanks for every part of your body
- Invest in a private yoga session
- Get a manicure or pedicure on a regular basis
- Put on a good song and dance to it
- Sleep in
- Get a massage
- Schedule a weekend away
- Take a bath with Epson salts, light a candle, read a good book, or play something soothing and uplifting
- Think of four ways you could treat yourself and do one each week
- Write in your gratitude journal
- Eat regular meals
- Watch a sunset
- Take a walk in the woods or on the beach
- Buy new lingerie
- Buy a new book and schedule uninterrupted time to read it
- Rent a boat and spend the day soaking up sunshine with family and friends
- Go to a concert or theatrical event you've wanted to see
- Begin a collection: stamps, thimbles, spoons, dolls, action figures, sports memorabilia, etc. – each time you achieve a goal, buy another item for your collection

- Throw a dinner party, cook your favourite healthy foods, and celebrate with friends
- Have a night out at the movies with a friend you haven't seen for a while
- Attend an art show or visit a gallery or local museum
- Go to your local amusement park and recapture the excitement you felt as a child

4. *Choose Tangible Ways to Celebrate Success and Reward Yourself Regularly*

Build on the momentum of your successes. As soon as you achieve one of your goals, take time to reward yourself in some way. Use music for motivation and rewards. Music is a great tool in fitness; it can provide a tempo for your gym workouts and crank up your energy during runs and walks.

5. *Be Proud of Yourself*

Assessing your results and setting new goals is a good strategy to follow. It's important to look for ongoing improvement in your health and fitness program. It's the highs that will take you through the lows. It's the commitment to keep going that will make your journey a success.

Identify your top accomplishments and your successes: the races you entered, the laps you swam in the pool, the hikes you completed, or the people you inspired and who inspired you. Look back on what you have achieved already. Reread the pages of your **FIT Workbook and Gratitude Journal**.

Our Turn...

Susan's Story

After my triumph in completing two full marathons – walking for seven and a half hours in each race – I started to analyze what I had achieved and how I could apply the lessons I learned to other aspects of my life. Over the past eight years since I completed my second marathon, I have learned many lessons about passion, hard work, continuous improvement, compassion, discipline, focus, perseverance, and hands-on dedication. I also learned to accept the limitations of my body and to celebrate every success, both big and small.

My rewards for committing to a healthier lifestyle include a stronger body, mental clarity and peace, celebrating with family and friends, new clothes, and massages. Since moving downtown and, with the help of daily-guided meditation, I have learned to be gentle with myself, to embrace nature and solitude, to relax, and to try to stay focused on the present.

One of the ways I reward myself is through travel. Taking care of my body and my mind has enabled me to plan and enjoy trips to interesting places that include hiking and walking.

Theresa's Story

Since our last book, I have achieved many great rewards in my fitness. For starters the three Guinness World Records for running the greatest distance in twelve hours on a treadmill. The fact that I am now training with an Olympic gold medalist is an incredible achievement and reward.

But actually the biggest achievement is that I am getting healthier and more knowledgeable about me as the years pass. I am taking on more and I have a stronger sense of me. The biggest reward is the confidence I now hold in the possibilities I can create for myself.

Your Turn...

Some ideas to get you started:

1. Write in your **FIT Workbook and Gratitude Journal**:
    *   How comfortable are you in celebrating your own successes and rewarding yourself?
    *   What have been your biggest fitness successes, achievements, and areas of progress?
    *   How will you celebrate your successes with tangible rewards?

- What will they be?
    - On a daily basis
    - On a weekly basis
    - On an on-going basis
    - When you achieve short-term goals
    - When you achieve long-term goals
    - When you achieve blue-sky goals

2. Add to your own **vision board**, illustrating your achievements and rewards.

3. **Use photography** to capture images of your achievements and rewards.

4. Turn to Appendix A, Step 9, to find tools designed by Catherine M. Sabiston and Eva Pila to help you plan your system of rewards.

Step 10. Assess Your Results, Imagine the Possibilities

"I think it's once in a lifetime that you get an opportunity like that, but over 750 gold medals are quite treasured – and I give my medals away. Because why do I need 800 medals? At this point, I know I'm going to get some more."

Olga Kotelko, 95

While Olga Kotelko said she's treasured all of her achievements, carrying the Olympic torch as part of the relay for the 2010 Vancouver Games was a particular standout.

Analyze Your Health, Fitness, Nutrition, and Spirituality Results

As with any other activity in your life, it's tempting to fall into a routine when it comes to health and fitness. That's actually all some people want: a routine that maintains their health, and that's great. There's no reason that everyone should be aiming to run marathons or enrol themselves in extreme fitness programs.

However, even the simple maintenance of health and fitness will require you to reassess your goals and activities and make adjustments. After all, the ways to maintain your fitness will change as you age and your life changes.

Realize how health and fitness empower you. Enjoy feeling more confidence, control, and motivation in maintaining your fitness and health once you start to see results.

Five Strategies for Evaluating Your Results and Setting New Goals

1. List Areas that Challenged You and the Lessons You Learned

Take time to examine the problems you have experienced and find ways to modify your expectations and your program in the future. Evaluate the type of plan that works for you and create strategies to work around your biggest obstacles.

2. *What Have You Achieved as a Result of Your Commitment to Health and Your Body?*

Reflect back on your biggest successes, achievements, and areas of progress. View your accomplishments from a positive perspective. When you are stressed, take stock as you communicate to yourself that being active and achieving a healthy lifestyle are truly important to you.

3. *Develop Long-Term Strategies to Evaluate Results and Set New Goals*

Assessing your results and setting new goals is a good strategy to follow. It's important to look for ongoing improvement in your health and fitness program. Share your goals with other people, including your support network, and ask for their support.

4. *Experiment with Different Kinds of Fitness Routines or Activities*

1. **Yoga-based fitness**:
   - Hatha
   - Vinyasa
   - Restorative yoga
   - Power yoga
   - Hot yoga
   - Yin yoga
   - Iyengar
   - YogaFit
   - Yoga fusion
   - Water yoga

2. **Movement-based fitness**:
   - Zumba classes: Set to fast and slow Latin rhythms, Zumba uses easy-to-follow moves and routines that include interval training and resistance training.
   - Nia: Express yourself with this free-form style of movement that balances out with technically precise moves – all designed to optimize your body, mind, emotions, and spirit.

- Cycle karaoke: Sing as you cycle.
- Trampoline: Jump to stay fit.

3. **Martial arts**:
   - Workouts like Kenpo increase muscle tone, flexibility, endurance, coordination, and speed. They create a feeling of focus in daily life, increased self-esteem, respect for self and others, and self-discipline.
   - Boxing and kickboxing are popular fitness programs, with classes and gyms available everywhere.

4. **High-speed fitness**:
   - Tabata: This high-intensity interval training was originally developed for Japan's Olympic skating team. It has become a favorite high-speed workout. It combines twenty seconds of intense workouts with ten seconds of rest in four-minute rounds.

5. **Weights-based fitness**:
   - Kettle bells: This is a popular Russian dumbbell workout. Although it may feel a bit like flinging a bowling ball around a room for thirty minutes, advocates say it's an incredible workout. A kettle bell looks like a cannonball with a handle. Using it combines cardiovascular, muscle strength, muscle endurance, and flexibility training in a program that is efficient and complete.

6. **Water-based fitness**:
   - Ai Chi: Slow-flowing movement through warm water is great for relaxation or stretching. Ai Chi is designed to strengthen and tone the body, while also promoting relaxation and a healthy mind-body relationship. The technique was developed in Japan in the1990s and is now practiced all over the world, particularly in North America.
   - Aqua jog: This is a high-intensity, low-impact aerobic workout in deep water designed to increase aerobic fitness, as well as tone and strengthen muscles.

- Arthritis aquatics: This type of class helps to improve joint flexibility and muscle strength.
- Water kickboxing: This is a low-impact, high-intensity aerobics program that incorporates kickboxing moves in the water.
- HydroRide: Spinning in the pool.

7. **For the adventurous**:
   - Paddle boarding
   - Mud runs
   - Extreme races
   - Skydiving
   - Mountain climbing
   - Marathons
   - Snowshoeing
   - Rock climbing
   - Zip-lining
   - Triathlon
   - Ironman
   - Cross fit

5. *Revise Your Health and Fitness Plan*

With your newfound self-awareness, confidence, and self-esteem, set new goals for the future. Encourage yourself to try new things and reach challenging goals. Revise your fitness plan. Whatever you decide from here, aim high. Consider:

- A fitness-focused event
- A fitness-based vacation
- Masters competitions

Our Turn...

Susan's Story

After completing two full marathons, I knew I had achieved something remarkable – twice – and was comfortable with not wanting to commit the time and effort to train for yet another one. I realized that I had rarely given my body credit for coming through for me and I now appreciate its capabilities.

I have taken a good look at my life and know that I cannot control the process of aging, but I can embrace my body and my health and stop the weight cycling that I have done for most of life. I understand that health and fitness do stretch well into later life and can offset symptoms of aging.

Being happy with my family, my work, my travel, my health, and my fitness all contribute to being happy with my body. I am more focused on real priorities, make better decisions, and feel connected with my inner self.

My blue-sky goals are to incorporate opportunities for kayaking and snorkelling into my life and to walk part of the Camino de Santiago trail in Spain.

Theresa's Story

My blue-sky goals will never stop. They are what fuel my inner spirit and bring me to life – give me direction and inspiration. My blue-sky goal is that by 2017 I am competing in the women's 100-meter Canadian masters, and aim to make it to the worlds. Also, I would love to learn to teach a few more classes, such as Zumba and yoga. The experience of being part of a group in action, and leading that group, is truly an inspiration and a wonderful way to connect.

Your Turn...

Some ideas to get you started:

1. Review your **Weekly FIT Training Log** and your **FIT Workbook and Gratitude Journal,** and write about your results and possibilities.
   - List your Successes.
   - Identify your top fitness accomplishments and successes, such as the races you entered, the laps you swam in the pool, the hikes you completed, and the people you

inspired and coached through your own health and fitness program.

- List the areas that challenged you and the lessons you learned.
- Evaluate your current goals and new goals that you would like to set.
- Name several blue-sky goals you would like to set that are adventurous and ambitious.
- What have you achieved more generally in your life as a result of your relationship with your body, health, and fitness?

2. Add your results and blue-sky goals to your **vision board**.
3. **Use photography** to capture images of your results and possibilities.
4. Turn to Appendix A, Step 10, to find Catherine M. Sabiston and Eva Pila's tools for a goal checkup and setting new goals.

PART 3

TECHNIQUES AND EXERCISES TO STRENGTHEN MIND, BODY, AND SOUL

by
The Art of Living Foundation's
Debra Joy Eklove and Nayna Trehan

"There are many mind-body programs and interventions. The Art of Living programs are the most comprehensive and effective programs that I have encountered. These experiential courses allow participants to interact dynamically with the body, breath, mind, intellect, and emotions, resulting in profound insights, awareness and behavior change.

"The self-care tools in The Art of Living programs allow participants to reap the long-term benefits for greater physical, mental, and emotional health. I recommend The Art of Living programs to clients of all ages who are ready to take the next step towards limitless potential."

Dr. Larissa Popov, Naturopathic Doctor

"When we think of optimal health, typically we think of physical health – being in the best possible shape. Even though our mental health determines so much about the quality of our life, rarely does it occur to us that we can also aim for optimal mental health. If we are stressed or unhappy, even if our body is in great shape we aren't going to enjoy our lives.

"We spend time improving nutrition, fine-tuning exercise regimes, perhaps even taking supplements and medications to improve how our body functions and especially for how our body looks and feels. In many ways, the same can be done for our mind.

"If we take the time to understand our mind and care for it – provide it with all the activities and ingredients it needs to function optimally – we can achieve a more resilient and lustrous mind. The Art of Living provides the means for everyone, through awareness, breathing, meditation and other practices, to achieve this often forgotten but hugely important skill of taking care of the mind."

Dr. Abhimanyu Sud, Medical Doctor

Understanding Stress – A Constructive Approach

Let's start with this understanding of stress:

Stress is what happens to our body and mind when our commitments and activities require more energy than we have to fulfill them.

Do you see how, when life has many demands and our energy level does not allow us to fulfill or meet them, this stress leads us to experience negative emotions such as anger, agitation, frustration, and anxiety? When such stress gets out of control, it can manifest as depression, illnesses, and even loss of hope or interest in life.

When we have enough energy, we meet and fulfill life's many demands with a positive attitude. How we manage this energy defines how we manage and relate to stress. The Sanskrit word for energy, or life force, is prana. When our prana is high, we can sail through all of our responsibilities and demands. We are uplifted by challenges and accomplishments. When prana is low, then even the smallest task can overwhelm or upset us, and sends us spiralling into negativity.

How to Increase Prana – Our Life Force Energy

Four Sources of Energy and How to Maximize their Benefits

1. Food
- Eat local, organic, fresh food.
- Eat the appropriate mixture of grains, fruits, vegetables, oils, and nuts.
- Eat proper amounts. Overeating makes the body and mind lethargic. Eating too little leaves us weak and frustrated.
- Eat at the right times of day: have your biggest meal of the day at noon.

2. Sleep and Exercise
- Going to sleep before midnight is beneficial to your whole system.
- Typically six to eight hours of uninterrupted sleep is what we need, and more as we age. Too much or too little makes us sluggish and grumpy.

- Prepare for sleep by calming down in advance, like the birds do.
- The right kind of exercise for our specific type of body and mind keeps us balanced and ready for sleep.

3. Breath

- Breathing is the most vital source of energy and is often ignored: without breath there is no life.
- Breathing exercises help enhance lung capacity and we have more energy. We typically only use a small percentage of our lung capacity.
- Using the breath, full slow breath, is one way to help detoxify the body and mind.

4. Meditative and Positive State of Mind

- Surrounding ourselves with positive people and healthy environments helps the mind to be positive and energized.
- Spiritual or uplifting music and books bring harmony to the mind.
- Spending time in nature has healing and rejuvenating effects.
- Daily meditation brings the mind into a deep state of calmness.
- As prana increases, stress reduces, the mind relaxes, and our capacity to be active and happy increases.

Five Strategies for Understanding the Mind and Breath, and Unlocking the Meditative State of Mind

1. Understand the Mind

Exercise to Experience the Nature of the Mind

Sit with your eyes closed. Let your mind go free and let your thoughts come without resisting them. Notice how your mind is either caught up in the past or in the future. The nature of the mind is to vacillate between the past and the future. It keeps us busy thinking about what happened in the past moment, day, or years, or the next moment, hour, day, month, or years.

You may have noticed how thoughts of the past often bring up sadness, anger, regret, and frustration. Thoughts of the future commonly bring up anxiety, uncertainty and fears.

However, where does life exist?
Are you living in the past or in the future?
Life is happening in the present!
And what is happening in the present moment?
In the present moment there is joy, happiness, peace, dynamism, confidence, and focus.

2. Understand the Breath

Breath is the most precious thing in life: without it there is no life. The very first action when we are born is a deep breath in, and a breath out is the last action. Between these is what we call life! Even though breath is so significant to our physical existence, unless we are running a marathon, chasing a bus, or in a severe condition we rarely ever think about it.

Every emotion has a corresponding rhythmic pattern in the breath. Notice what happens to your breath when you are angry: it becomes short and shallow. Notice what happens to your breath when you are happy and relaxed: it becomes slow and deep.

Usually our emotions influence the breath. However, we can learn to reverse the cycle by learning specific rhythmic breathing techniques that can influence and change our emotions and state of mind. This brings the power to improve our emotions and be in control.

The Art of Living's Happiness Program includes a scientifically-validated ancient breathing practice called Sudarshan Kriya Yoga™ (SKY). The SKY practice helps to restore our natural biorhythms so that we may experience peace and happiness. Many toxins in the body are released through the breath. The SKY practice helps to release emotional and physical stresses, transforming our perception of life into a more positive state. One SKY practitioner, Filiz Odabas-Geldiay, says of the program:

"Sudarshan Kriya was a lifesaver for me in recovering from fibromyalgia – a painful muscle disorder that was triggered by a car accident twenty years ago. With a newborn and a toddler to care for, I fell into a depression when my doctor said there is no cure for it and that I have to learn to live with it. Fortunately, the universe had other plans for me. What physical therapy sessions and cortisone shots didn't heal in one and a half years, practicing the powerful breathing technique of SKY did in one and a half months. I have been free of fibromyalgia ever since."

3. Practice Yoga

Yoga helps to release tensions in the body and brings the mind into a stable and calm state. Art of Living Yoga is a complete practice that involves asanas (postures), breathing, meditation, and time-tested wisdom.

Here are ten steps to release tension and stress from your body. These steps form a subtle yogic sequence. You can do these exercises anytime, anywhere to help release tension and stress from your body. Take a few minutes at home, at your workstation or when traveling and feel the results.

Step 1: Place your right palm on top of your head. Using gentle pressure, make circles on your scalp, massaging first in one direction then the other.

Step 2: Place both palms on the sides of your head above the ears and massage the sides of the head with gentle circles, first in one direction, then the other.

Step 3: Iron out your forehead. Place the fingertips of each hand in the middle of the forehead and gently, at the same time, move fingers of both hands in an outward direction across your forehead.

Step 4: Relax the eyebrows. Using your index finger and thumb, pinch your eyebrows five to six times, starting above the nose, moving in the outward direction.

Step 5: Relax the eyes. Roll your eyes five to six times clockwise and then anti-clockwise without moving your head. Squeeze your eyes tight and then open them wide. Repeat this ten to fifteen times.

Step 6: Relax the ears. Using both hands at the same time pull both ears from the top, side and bottom for ten to fifteen seconds.

Step 7: Relax the jaw. Place three fingers on each cheek, near the jaw. Open your mouth, and using your fingers, massage and iron out the knots in the jaw area, moving back and forth along the teeth line, the jaw, and in downward strokes from jaw to chin. Then, gently open and close your mouth eight to ten times.

Step 8: Relax the neck. Stretch your neck gently, with great care not to strain. If you have neck problems consult a professional before doing this. Breathing in, take your chin up and head back. Breathing out, bring your chin to the chest. Rotate your chin and head in a clockwise direction. Breathe in as you go up and breathe out as you go down. Then reverse the direction of rotation. If any place is painful, pause and slowly breathe into that place and then continue.

Step 9: Relax the shoulders. Use both your hands to massage your neck and shoulders, with pressure that is comfortable for you. Raise the shoulders, and let them drop and make the sound "ha."

Step 10: Gently rotate your shoulders moving them forward, up, back, and down, gently squeezing your shoulder blades together when you go back. Breathe in as you go up and breathe out as you go down. Do this five to six times and then reverse the direction again. Repeat five or six times.

4. *Practice The Art of Living Meditation*

Meditation is getting in touch with your deeper self. The quality of rest and renewal from a few minutes of meditation is deeper than rest acquired from sleep. To give yourself the best meditation experience, note the following:

- It is best to practice meditation on an empty stomach, before breakfast, lunch, or dinner. If you have eaten, wait two to three hours after a full meal, or thirty minutes after a snack.
- Meditate sitting in a comfortable position, with your spine straight and mind alert. It can be on a chair, or sitting on the floor. A clean place, even with flowers or a candle, helps set a fresh and pleasant atmosphere.
- The effects of meditation grow when done regularly. Meditate at least once a day for twenty minutes, if possible in the same place. When you are new to meditation take the forty-day challenge – commit to meditating for forty continuous days. Then you will have the experience of its impact.

A Four Step Exercise for Meditation Practice

Step 1: Find a comfortable space for yourself, ideally with some fresh air. Turn off your phone. Remove as many distractions as possible, like pets, music, or TV.

Step 2: Plan to sit for twenty minutes, come what may. For these twenty minutes sit comfortably, with the spine straight, with the intention of applying the following three principles in a very light manner:

1. I want nothing.
2. I do nothing.
3. I am nothing.

During meditation, if you find your mind wandering, bring these intentions back again in a light manner.

Step 3: Close your eyes and let go. Hands rest comfortably on the knees, palms facing up. Whatever thoughts or feeling or sensations come, just let them be, without giving them any importance.

Step 4: When complete, gently take a few deep breaths and open your eyes. Smile. Take a few moments sitting with eyes open, and again take a few breaths before slowly standing.

Guided Meditations can also be very effective. For guided meditations by The Art of Living Foundation, download the Sattva app, available from both the Apple App Store and Android Play Store at www.sattva.life.

5. Create Your Own Daily Meditation Log

Use a calendar or a journal and mark each day you complete your twenty-minute meditation. Write some impressions from your experience. Complete your daily meditation for forty straight days. If you miss a day start counting from the beginning. After forty days observe the effects, any changes in your behavior and state of mind.

Reported Benefits of Meditation

Using the above techniques and the SKY practice, you can unlock the fourth source of energy: a meditative state of mind. People who have used these techniques report:

- Reduced stress, anxiety, and anger
- Greater sense of joy, happiness, and enthusiasm
- Inner confidence
- Strength and skill to break through personal barriers
- Improved interpersonal skills
- Increased energy
- Higher productivity

A meditative, happy, and calm mind is able to make better decisions. This helps us be more creative and live a healthier, more positive, and productive life.

Understanding Ayurveda – The Science of Life

Ayurveda – the science of life – is a medical and wellness system that dates back to 5000 years ago. It has much to offer to our modern lives. The World Health Organization recognizes ayurvedic medicine as one of the oldest systems of medicine in the world.

The aim of ayurveda is to maintain a person's health and prevent and cure diseases. Yoga, meditation, and diet are some of the tools and techniques used by ayurveda practitioners. Ayurveda describes the beneficial, non-beneficial, happy, and unhappy aspects of life.

A crucial feature of ayurveda is in recognizing how each of us has a unique constitution. Understanding this explains how people respond to and benefit from different foods, exercise, work, and social interactions. Our unique constitution is physical and mental. It is based on the unique combination of five elements in our system: space, air, fire, water, and earth. To gain a sense of your constitution, imagine and describe your body with the elements as follows:

- All our bones are solid, and are the earth element.
- All the fluids in the body are the water element.
- Digestion, temperature regulation, and sight all require light or heat, and are the fire element.
- Breath comes in and out of our lungs, and is the air element.
- Hollow areas and joints in the body are necessary openings for movement, and these are the space element.

Just like our bodies, the whole world is made up of only these elements. Understanding the qualities of the elements, how they are affecting our mental and physical health, and how we can keep them in a healthy balance is ayurveda.

In ayurveda, balance refers to the unique combination of the five elements in you at birth. This combination is considered a gift that provides the tools you need for your unique life journey, and to achieve life's ultimate goal, which in ayurveda is spiritual development and consciousness.

Dosha

Your constitution is described by the term dosha. The doshas are:

• Vata (air and space)
• Pitta (fire and water)
• Kapha (water and earth)

Some people thrive on a cold day – they may have more fire in their constitution and be pitta. Some people have great stamina – they may have more earth or water in their constitution and be kapha. Some people are very creative and unpredictable – they may have more air and space in their constitution and be vata. You may be one, two, or a combination all three doshas, depending on personal qualities and characteristics.

Many websites offer quizzes or questionnaires that can help discern your dosha. The best way to learn one's dosha is to have a consultation with an ayurveda practitioner who is trained to read your unique pulse.

Once we know our dosha we can better understand how daily activities impact us physically, mentally, emotionally, and spiritually. We can consciously make decisions about lifestyle, work, food, and recreation to help maximize our health, and lead productive and fulfilling lives. An aim in Ayurveda is to encourage choices that keep the quality of our mind as calm and joyful as possible, so we make the best decisions, and stay positive and stress free.

The mind vacillates constantly. It can be sattvic (calm and joyful), rajasic (agitated and moving), or tamasic (sleepy and lethargic). All three conditions are necessary parts of life, and we move among them.

Choices we make with diet, lifestyle, friends, and work do affect our strength and balance. Ayurveda provides tools to help us increase our sattva and happiness as much as possible. In Ayurveda, diet plays an important role. The Art of Wholesome Eating is a fun and interactive program designed to tickle your taste buds and give you the knowledge to awaken successfully for your own health needs.

To learn more about this outstanding wellness system, Sri Sri Ayurveda offers educational programs in towns and cities throughout the world. At its main site at the International Art of Living Center in Saint-Mathieu-du-Parc, Quebec, ayurvedic retreats – using yoga and ayurvedic tools of massage, diet, and rest – are offered to support the return to energy and vitality. For more information and available programs through The Art of Living, visit: srisriayurveda.ca.

The Bigger Impact – Peace

The first step to a peaceful world is to become peaceful yourself. On the United Nations International Peace Day, Sri Sri Ravi Shankar, Founder of The Art of Living Foundation, wrote:

> *"We all have the responsibility of bringing peace to every nook and corner of the world. Unless every member of our global family is peaceful, our peace is incomplete. Peace is needed at three levels: first is inner peace, which is of the mind. It brings dynamism in our action and makes us more powerful. The second level is peace in our immediate environment, our family, friends, and workplace. The third level is peace between nations and continents, which is most important."*

Take responsibility for your own happiness. Come what may – keep yourself happy. Be happy!

The Art of Living Programs

- Art Excel Program (ages 8–13): Learn breathing exercises, yoga, and meditation paired with the "six golden keys to success."
- Happiness Program (ages 18+): Learn the Sudarshan Kriya (SKY) practice to restore life's natural rhythm of happiness.

- Art of Meditation Program (ages 17+): Learn a simple but powerful personalized technique called sahaj samadhi to meditate on your own.
- Art of Living Yoga Program (all ages): Learn a pure and authentic form of yoga for beginners and seekers.

Research on The Art of Living practices can be found at www.aolresearch.org.

Our Turn...

Debra Joy Eklove's Story

Many years ago I was told my body was blocking natural reflexes. This began my quest to understand and learn about my body, mind, and spirit. My passion became teaching peace, in workshops and with clients.

My first Art of Living program in 2002 was a key to a world full of insights and celebrations, to people from all backgrounds, cultures, and traditions who value making the world a better place. Our programs and courses help me apply my talents, skills, and interests to meaningful tasks, and to focus on developing inner peace as a key to world peace.

Nayna Trehan's Story

My mother forced me, a rebellious teenager at the time, to take The Art of Living youth program. It taught me how to handle my emotions and keep my mind stable through the challenges of school and home. Further programs helped me become a strong community leader. I started to feel joy in giving, rather than only taking. The Art of Living program made me realize not only the love and joy inside, but also a greater cause in life. Breathing exercises and meditation are a core part of my life now and I feel equipped to take anything on!

Victoria Block's Story (Art of Living Participant)

How has spirituality helped to empower me as a woman? I have been on a spiritual path for so long that sometimes I forget that I am a woman, a person, on this path. It is difficult to say which has helped the most: the constant awareness of the course points, or the delicious meditations, which have opened up some other realm for me. All of the practices bring you towards the present moment. With less stuff pulling you down, this present moment becomes so full and miraculous. This creation is a miracle. How is it possible that we are not constantly in awe?

Marcy Jackson's Story (Art of Living Participant)

For the past twenty-seven years Sudarshan Kriya has had a positive impact and enhanced my life physically, mentally, emotionally, and spiritually. My life has been transformed into a state of awareness and alertness. It matters not what I am doing, whether walking in the woods, sitting in an airplane, skiing mountainous peaks, dealing with challenges, or looking at a rose – life is lived more fully and it makes me feel contented and smile from my heart. The skills learned in the course enable me to be in the present moment, to cope with the unexpected and better support those around me.

Your Turn...

Start your own daily meditation log, and use a calendar or journal to mark each day you complete your twenty-minute meditation. Write down impressions from your experience.

PART 4

EATING FOR VIGOR AND VITALITY

by
Kirsten Bedard
Ladylean.com

When Susan and Theresa asked me to take part in writing this book, I was honored and immediately agreed. Their first book, *Power Source for Women: Proven Fitness Strategies, Tools, and Success Stories for Women 45+*, has inspired thousands of women to make positive changes to their eating and activity habits. It fills a void in the plethora of diet plans and exercise programs where the discussion of how to successfully devise and implement enduring habits is often overlooked. Understanding our motivations is vital to the longevity of any positive lifestyle habit.

I have been working in the field of food and nutrition for over twenty years, helping people lower cholesterol, maximize performance, and boost energy. Regardless of what their needs are, the solution lies in clearly understanding the complex interrelationship between the brain, body, nutrients, and blood.

We can all agree with certainty that we need food for energy. Yet that's not why we most often eat. Let's be honest – we love food. While there's no arguing that energy is the reason why we must eat, the joy found in cooking, smelling, and sharing food is why we love to eat. Food is exciting, entertaining, enlivening, exotic, enlightening, and yes, even erotic.

So it is fair to say that food is energy and food is enjoyment. We want to have both. Of course we do. The trouble is that the two motivating forces for eating do not always blend well together. Were we to eat for energy's sake alone, we might bore our palates, leave our bellies yearning, and our urges unsatisfied. On the other hand, were we to eat without being mindful and listening to our body's hunger and satiety cues, we would soon find our health suffering and our well-being wavering.

The Dichotomy of Food

The way we eat directly affects our health but, more significantly, our brain – how we think and feel – which in turn influences how we move and care for our body. Food not only fuels the body in which we live, but it is the one and only form of fuel for our brain as well. What we eat has a profound impact on our motivation and how we live our lives. Since the brain is the driving force for everything that takes place with and within the body, it is the brain on which our vigor and vitality depend. What is good for the brain is good for the body.

I spend much time explaining carbohydrates, clarifying the science and how carbs affect the brain and energy levels. Why? Because carbohydrates can – and do – create problems in the body. While in the past it may not have been of much importance to understand the science of the foods we were eating, it is now. We live in a culture where we are constantly bombarded by food and food marketing. We are fed an endless stream of information and misinformation telling us truths, quasi-truths, and untruths. And not surprisingly, we eat a whole lot of them.

The Trouble with Carbohydrates

Carbohydrates are easy to package, produce, and transport, and with their long shelf lives and addictive qualities, they are highly profitable. The more we eat them, the more we crave them. They flood our grocery stores and kitchen cupboards, make up our lunches and snacks, dominate our dinners and drinks. We eat them in glorious abundance.

The number one reason for our inclination to carbohydrates is a five-letter word: s-u-g-a-r. All carbohydrates break down into sugar – from bread to pasta, whole grains to legumes. Glucose is the primary sugar in all of these foods, and our greatest concern. Even quinoa and oats are made up of sugar – glucose.

Blood Sugar and the Brain

The second reason for our inclination to carbohydrates is another five-letter word: b-r-a-i-n. The brain loves sugar... for a brief few minutes... until it panics at the high amount of sugar racing into the bloodstream. When blood sugar is high, the brain sends insulin out to dump that sugar into fat cells, and low blood sugar follows. Low blood sugar in turn causes the brain to panic – again – and it summons cortisol this time, which leads to cravings for more carbohydrates, inflammation, and more serious problems follow.

It is important to eat mindfully. Whether we want to boost energy levels, run faster, or improve any aspect of our health, stabilizing blood sugar is the first step.

Five Strategies for Stabilizing Blood Sugar

1. Eat Vegetables

For most of us, stabilizing blood sugar levels means cutting back on the amount of glucose we are eating. Cutting back on the amount of dense carbohydrates – grains and processed grains – is a strategic way to cut back on both sugar and calories. The smartest and simplest way to do this is to choose vegetables.

Let's be clear about something here, we always need some carbohydrates. The key is to be picky about which ones we are eating regularly – what we want is maximum nutrition for the least amount of sugar. Dense glucose carbohydrates – like grains – are high in glucose and proportionally low in nutrients. Vegetables are the exact opposite.

Vegetables get the vote in the campaign for energy and well-being. The leafy green and cruciferous types, in particular, contain very small amounts of glucose, but are rich in vitamins, minerals, fibre and water. They can be eaten leisurely and in abundance.

2. Counterbalance Carbohydrates with Protein and Fat

Think of a tightrope walker, trying to get from one end of the rope to the other without crashing to the ground. She uses a counterbalance to keep steady as she moves across the rope. Carbohydrates are like the tightrope walker traveling through the bloodstream. Protein and fat act as the counterbalance. They help prevent both the spike – and then the crash – that carbohydrates can create. They ensure food is burned as fuel, not stored as fat.

Protein and fat help to slow down the absorption of food from the intestines into the bloodstream. They temper the flow of sugar entering the blood, since they take a longer time to be broken down and absorbed. Protein and fat also satiate our hunger for longer periods.

Protein as a Transformer

Protein is made up of amino acids that are linked together in food, broken apart during digestion, and then re-assembled in the body as needed. Amino acids nourish the brain, act as enzymes, and repair all of our cells and tissues. During long bouts of activity, protein is versatile and able to transform into whatever the body needs.

How Much Protein – And What Type?

Eggs, chicken, meat, fish, cottage cheese, Greek yogurt, and protein powders are all good sources of protein. Small amounts of protein, a few times per day, even as snacks, can contribute to a nourished body and mind.

What if You're a Vegetarian?

Not wanting to consume animal products is understandable. There are two things to be cautious about if you're a vegetarian. First, some of the amino acids are essential, meaning the body can't produce them on its own. Having a vegan protein shake is a simple way to get these into your diet. Second, consider increasing the quantity of fat in meals and snacks. Avocados, nuts, and oils help to keep your blood sugar levels stable.

3. Eat Fat to Win the Fuel Race

Speaking of fat, do you remember the tale of the tortoise and the hare? The hare challenges the tortoise to a race. Reluctantly, the tortoise agrees. (It doesn't much like to race). When the gun goes off, the hare bounds out in front, sprinting ahead, leaping along... until he crashes, not even halfway to the finish. Flat out of energy already, the hare lies down for a nap. The tortoise, on the other hand, moves along, smooth and steady, straight to the finish line. Winner!

Both fat (the tortoise) and carbohydrates (the hare) are forms of fuel, and fats are often the most sustainable choices for the long haul. Slow and steady wins the race. Fat provides us with more sustainable energy compared to carbohydrates. Because of this, the brain prefers fat rather than carbohydrates as optimal fuel.

4. Don't Jack Your Blood Sugar at Breakfast!

We wake up in the morning, not having eaten for many hours, and we can be fairly certain that our blood sugar is dipping down pretty low. Tiptoe cautiously, to gently rouse blood sugar – and your brain – back up to a balanced state. You don't want to wind it up like Jack-in-the-box. When your blood sugar is low, you are especially sensitive to the impacts of a high carbohydrate meal.

Best Bets for Breakfast

- Two eggs, cooked greens, tomato slices, 1 tablespoon olive oil
- A protein shake: 1 cup unsweetened almond milk, ½ cup fruit, 1 tablespoon flax seeds, and 25 grams protein powder
- 1 cup cottage cheese or Greek yogurt, ½ cup fruit, and 1 tablespoon ground flax seeds

5. Eat Snacks to Keep You Steady

If we've had the right fuel for breakfast, we should be contentedly cruising through the morning, towards lunch, insulin at bay, energy constant, the mind clear, and moods level – all signs that breakfast is being burned as fuel rather than stored as fat. We may not even feel hungry.

A key strategy for stable blood sugar is to eat every three hours. This means eating something before you're hungry. Once hunger has struck, your blood sugar has already taken a nosedive. By then, it's too late. Cortisol will be screaming at you for sugar. Don't wait for that crash. It only makes it harder.

Snacks are like training wheels. Their purpose is to keep us steady and prevent the crash. Protein and fat prevent blood sugar drops and minimize cravings, allowing calories to be released from fat and burned as fuel.

By the time we've crashed, it's too late. Remember this. We want to prevent that drop. A mid-morning snack means we make it to lunch in a rational, reasonable state of mind. It's easier to make wise lunch choices if blood sugar hasn't hit rock bottom when the bell rings.

Snacks as Keepers of the Peace

Another way to think of snacks is as peacekeepers. They keep our brain feeling safe and secure – at ease, free of toil and trouble. Both high and low blood sugar disrupt mental peace, setting off the brain's panic alarm, and sending insulin and cortisol racing out to protect the body. Snacks help keep the brain on even keel. The brain has to be relaxed – alert and focused, yes, but calm. The purpose of snacks is to keep the brain chugging along smoothly throughout the day.

Five Snacks to Eat

- ½ avocado
- A boiled egg and an apple
- ½ cup cottage cheese
- Half a breakfast protein shake – other half in the afternoon
- 30 grams 85% dark chocolate

Summary of Stabilizing Blood Sugar

What we eat every day does affect how we act, think, and feel. Nutritionally, eating for stable blood sugar is the most important thing we can do for our health – and for our energy levels. When our blood sugar levels are stable, the brain is calm and clear since sugar is not racing through the bloodstream causing havoc.

Carbohydrates are not harmful when enjoyed in small amounts. A baguette can be a delightful treat now and again. The occasional indulgence is not a problem. The real concern is in our daily habits – and often those we think to be healthful. When carbohydrates are traded in for eggs and avocado, after a single week most people experience increased energy levels through the day.

Stable blood sugar is the foundation of eating for energy. It is pinnacle to our well-being, our motivation, and the proper functioning of our body and brain.

My Turn…

Kirsten's Story

As early as my high school days, I became interested in understanding food chemistry and how it either improved health or hindered it. I began personal training in university, because I've always been active and strong and I know that physical activity offers rewards, both mentally and physically. The more I understood how drastically eating and exercise impacted everything in the body, the clearer my mission became. I would coach and teach people **how** to eat and **why**. It was not something that could be left in the hands of marketing or magazines. While it is a complex science, the information is vital to living well and enjoying life. One of the only things we have control over with regards to our health is how we choose to eat and how we choose to move.

Your Turn…

1. Write in your **FIT Workbook and Journal** and answer these questions:
    *   Can you schedule two hours into the week to write a grocery list (divided by protein, fat, carbohydrates, and vegetables), shop, then wash and prep food for the week?
    *   What obstacles often get in the way of eating at regular intervals throughout the day to keep blood sugar levels steady? Can you carry nuts with you or stock your office or car with snacks?
    *   Can you experiment with new vegetables and recipes to bring some curiosity and creativity back into cooking and eating more vegetables?

- Knowing that protein is important for ongoing energy, and sources are limited, what are some simple strategies for having ready to eat protein on hand?
- How can you change your habits to align eating with energy while still finding food enjoyable?

2. Add to your own **vision board** to reflect your thoughts and feelings about food as nourishment for your mind, body, and spirit.

3. **Use photography** to capture images about food as nourishment.

Conclusion

Susan Sommers

After completing two marathons, I was excited to discover that I no longer felt as if I ever needed to do another. I knew I had achieved something remarkable and fulfilled a blue-sky goal. Each year I commit to completing one 10K race and one half-marathon, which are realistic, achievable goals for me.

I appreciate the fact that my current fitness program enables me to feel fit, control my weight, reduce stress, gain energy, and stay present. I have transformed my body and my health through weight training, walking, jogging, swimming, meditation, and stretching. I am proud of the way I look and feel and celebrate my successes.

Theresa Dugwell

Today my journey in life continues to find time for exercise. It is my number one priority, my life force, and my superpower. It energizes everything else in my life. I am a healthier, happier, and better person for me, and for others, because of making my health #1.

Today I am proud to say that I hold three Guinness World Records for running the greatest distance on a treadmill in twelve hours. I have completed twenty-one marathons, teach indoor cycling classes, and mentor women of all ages to take on the challenge of becoming the best they can be. I help women find their own superpower and celebrate who they are.

APPENDIX A

SELF-ASSESSMENT TOOLS, EXERCISES, AND QUIZZES

by Dr. Catherine M. Sabiston and Eva Pila[8]
University of Toronto

Step 1. Gain the Motivation You Need to Change

Decisional Balance

What are the advantages and disadvantages of making a change? Brainstorm what you think will be the most challenging health or body acceptance change for you. Use this worksheet to better understand and balance the advantages and disadvantages of making this change.

Table 1: The Advantages and Disadvantages of Making a Change[9]

+ Advantages of making change	− Disadvantages of making change
− Disadvantages of **not** making change	+ Advantages of **not** making change

Discover Your Motivation

One of the most important parts of fostering your motivation to be physically active is to understand why you want to be active and reflect on what you have done in the past. Think about some of the changes you have made to your lifestyle or to yourself in the past and answer the following:

Habits I have changed before:
1.
2.
3.

Things that helped me succeed:
1.
2.
3.

Strategies to overcome obstacles:
1.
2.
3.

Self-Talk to Discover Your Motivation

Self-talk can be very useful for increasing motivation, focusing attention, and discovering inspiration for your desired behavior change. Each of us carries an internal monologue throughout the day. We are more aware of self-talk after we have done something out of the ordinary, but it goes on most of the time. Unfortunately, most of us use self-talk to be critical of ourselves for things we have said or done that we wish were different. However, research shows that deliberately saying positive things to ourselves about our actions or intended actions can help build self-esteem and change ourselves for the better.

Can you think of anything positive you have said to yourself or others recently about becoming more physically active? Say them again. And again. It should feel good because they are real and positive things about you. Take a few minutes to write more positive statements that you could say to help motivate yourself to exercise before a planned session and help you feel good as you're engaging in the session. Positive self-statements should be brief and meaningful:

Post these statements on your mirror, fridge, or another place where you're likely to see them. Don't be afraid to say them to yourself! Positive self-talk can be motivating and encouraging – great for beginning a lifestyle change – and can lead to better self-esteem – great always!

Four Ways to Change Self-Talk

1. **Stop your thoughts**
   As soon as a negative thought emerges, use a cue to stop the thought before it continues. Cues that are often chosen include saying the word "stop" or snapping your fingers.

2. **Change negatives to positives**
   When a negative thought is stopped, it can instantly be changed into a positive statement (e.g. "I can't" is instantly replaced with "I can!" or "This will never work" to "This will work!")

3. **Countering**
   Instead of changing the wording of the thought only, another positive statement follows (e.g. "I can't run fast" but "I can run longer!"). The key here is that the positive statement has to be truthful, believable, and achievable.

4. **Reframing**
   Change the entire perspective. For example, rather than seeing a chance to fail – choose to focus on the opportunities to achieve!

Step 2. Tap into Your Passion

Reflect on your reasons for wanting to become physically active, and you will discover things that inspire you. What are your three most important reasons for wanting to do more physical activity?

1.
2.
3.

What are some of the things you hope will happen by doing more physical activity?

1.

2.

3.

Using the scale below, rate how you see your ability to make a lasting change to your physical activity?

1	2	3	4	5	6	7

not at all   completely

How do you think you could go about increasing your physical activity?

1.

2.

3.

Imagine

The use of imagery involves focusing all the sense to create or re-create experiences in the mind. Imagery can be used as a motivational and inspirational tool, as a relaxation tool, and as a method of improving performance.

Example

Imagine the example situation below and provide as much detail from your imagination as possible to make the image seem real:

> Select a specific exercise skill or activity. Imagine yourself performing the skill or activity in the place where you would normally practice, without anyone else present. Now close your eyes for about one minute and try to see yourself at this place, hear the sounds, feel the body movements, and be aware of your mood.

Step 3. Do Your Research

Research for Your Activity Toolbox

What behavioral tools have you acquired to help motivate yourself to be physically active?

1.
2.
3.
4.
5.

What do you need to learn or research to continue to progress towards your goals?

1.
2.
3.
4.
5.

Step 4. Surround Yourself with Supporters

To better understand the kind of social support you are receiving, it is useful to assess your level of support using a questionnaire. Read each definition of the type of support being considered and respond to the question accordingly.[10]

1. **Listening support**: *People who listen to you without giving advice or being judgmental*

   a) How many individuals provide you with listening support?

0–1	2–3	4–5	6–7	8 or more

   b) In general, how satisfied are you with the overall quality of listening support you receive?

1	2	3	4	5
very dissatisfied				very satisfied

c) How difficult would it be for you to obtain more listening support?

1	2	3	4	5
very dissatisfied				very satisfied

2. **Task challenge**: *People who challenge your way of thinking about your work or activity in order to stretch you, motivate you, and lead you to greater creativity, excitement, and involvement in your work or activity.*

a) How many individuals provide you with task challenge support?

0–1	2–3	4–5	6–7	8 or more

b) In general, how satisfied are you with the overall quality of task challenge support you receive?

1	2	3	4	5
very dissatisfied				very satisfied

c) How difficult would it be for you to obtain more task challenge support?

1	2	3	4	5
very dissatisfied				very satisfied

3. **Emotional support**: *People who comfort you and indicate to you that they are on your side and care for you.*

a) How many individuals provide you with emotional support?

0–1	2–3	4–5	6–7	8 or more

b) In general, how satisfied are you with the overall quality of emotional support you receive?

1	2	3	4	5
very dissatisfied				very satisfied

c) How difficult would it be for you to obtain more emotional support?

1	2	3	4	5
very dissatisfied				very satisfied

4. **Reality confirmation**: *People who are similar to you – see things the way you do – who help you confirm your perceptions and perspectives of the world and help you keep things in focus.*

a) How many individuals provide you with reality confirmation support?

0–1	2–3	4–5	6–7	8 or more

b) In general, how satisfied are you with the overall quality of reality confirmation support you receive?

1	2	3	4	5
very dissatisfied				very satisfied

c) How difficult would it be for you to obtain more reality confirmation support?

1	2	3	4	5
very dissatisfied				very satisfied

5. **Tangible assistance**: *People who provide you with financial assistance, products, or gifts.*

   a) How many individuals provide you with tangible assistance support?

0–1	2–3	4–5	6–7	8 or more

   b) In general, how satisfied are you with the overall quality of tangible assistance support you receive?

1	2	3	4	5
very dissatisfied				very satisfied

   c) How difficult would it be for you to obtain more tangible assistance support?

1	2	3	4	5
very dissatisfied				very satisfied

Take a few minutes to think about your answers and the amount of social support you are receiving. Reflect on some ways that you can use this support to help you reach your physical activity goals. Make a plan to invite a few people in your social network to become part of your physical activity plan. Write their initials and a specific role for them to play.

Role: _____ Supporter Initials: ____

Role: _____ Supporter Initials: ____

Role: _____ Supporter Initials: ____

Now contact these individuals and invite them to be a part of your support network!

Step 5. Believe You Can Achieve Your Goals

Exercise Activity Log

The first step in changing your activity level is to become more aware of what activities you are currently doing. Research has shown that one of the best ways to become more aware of how much or how little activity we do is by actually writing down information about our activities in a logbook. Take this first step in changing your behavior by writing down your activities in your training log.

In the next week, take some time to record the following in a journal or logbook:

a) What physical activities you did that lasted ten minutes or longer
b) How long you did each activity
c) How much effort it took to perform the activity using a 1 to 10 intensity scale
d) How many steps you did each day

Next step: set a personalized activity goal!

Purpose of Goal Setting

Goals provide you with a map of where you want to go, and how you plan to get there. Goals help to enhance commitment, effectiveness, efficiency, confidence, and motivation by setting a concrete plan that will streamline your efforts and allow you to see real progress.

There are three kinds of goals:

1. **Outcome**: e.g. completing a race
2. **Performance**: e.g. improving a walk time, lifting more weight
3. **Process**: e.g. walking ten minutes, three times a day; eating five to seven fruits and vegetables

Process goals are needed to succeed at the outcome goals, and they provide you with more opportunities to reflect on your progress, alter your goals as needed, and ultimately succeed at the outcome.

Build Steppingstones to Major Goals

A goal is something that we strive for and want to accomplish. For example, wanting to get stronger or to lose weight are goals. Unfortunately, these goals are long-term and general which makes it hard to create a specific plan of action. So, we need to set more specific, short-term goals.

If your goal is to achieve something by the end of the winter months, make smaller, progressive goals for each month that will put you on track to achieving the larger goal. If you have monthly short-term goals, you may even want to break these down into weekly goals, and goals for each day or exercise session, so that you are always focused and working on some component of your larger goal.

Start With a Short-Term Goal

Start by setting a specific goal that you will try to achieve by using the FITT principle (frequency, intensity, type, time). Your goal is to increase something that you are currently doing. Choose **one part** of the FITT principle to focus on and set your specific goal. Write your goal in the space below.

F   (frequency)
I   (intensity)
T   (type)
T   (time)

My goal is to:

Sign here: _____

Another principle for goal setting is to make your goals SMART (specific, measurable, achievable, realistic and resourced, time limited). Write your SMART goals in the space provided below.

Specific: Be very clear in what you want to achieve. Consider breaking the goal down into smaller steps. Example: "I will walk around the block."

Measurable: How will you know when you have achieved your goal? What will you be doing at that time? What will be different? What will you have started or be doing regularly? Example: "I will walk around the block for twenty minutes, three days per week."

Achievable: Ensure your goals are not too high. Consider setting smaller goals on your way to the big one. Celebrate your successes. If you don't achieve what you set out to do, then ask what you could do differently, what would help you succeed next time? Example: "I will walk around the block with my friend and will schedule and mark the day in my calendar.

Realistic and resourced: Is this achievable with the resources you have? Are there any other resources you need before you can achieve your goal? How can you access these resources? What problems might you have? What can you do to minimize those problems? Example: "I will walk around the block at a moderate pace."

Time Limited: Set a reasonable time limit to achieve your goal. One week, one month, six months, one year, five years? Consider smaller time limits for smaller steps. Example: "I will start my goal in two days and will evaluate my progress in two weeks."

Step 6. Develop Habits and Routines Aligned with Your Goals

How Emotion Regulation Supports Habits and Routines

One of the greatest challenges to maintaining our habits and routines may be mood – or how we are feeling at a certain time – and how that may impact our ability to reach our goals. It can be very helpful to keep track of your moods and emotions, and form strategies for managing and regulating moods to keep your new habits and routines on track.

Emotion regulation tools may be helpful. The basic principle is easy: minimize the negative emotions and maximize the positive ones. Step one is to track emotions with a mood diary to help you recognize what things and environments make you feel proud and happy (positive emotions) and what makes you feel tense, frustrated, or angry (negative emotions). Step two is to manage moods and emotions with breathing exercises, positive self-talk, laughter, and outings.

Mood Diary[11]

Day/Time	Mood/Emotion	Intensity of Mood/Emotion (0–100%)	Details of Mood (What was happening, where, with whom? What went through your mind? What were you doing just before and after you felt this?)

Tools to Regulate Mood

Increased awareness of your emotions can help to manage the good and the bad:

1. When you feel a negative mood or emotion coming on, stop what you are doing for a moment, close your eyes if you can, and breathe. Take a few deep breaths through your nose and exhale through the mouth. Simple, deep breathing works quickly and in the moment.
2. Practice positive self-talk.
3. Laugh more often and the louder the better! Laughter has been linked to many benefits, including lower stress, better mood, heightened immunity, and even reduced pain.
4. Take yourself outside, enjoy walking around the shopping malls, purposefully park the car in the furthest spots available – take advantage of lifestyle activities since any physical activity is good for your mood.

Become mindful and conscious of your emotions, focus only on what you can control, and use strategies to self-regulate so that you can live in the moment, with less stress.

Step 7. Create Your Own Action Plan

Creating an action plan can help you achieve your goals and track your progress. Use this worksheet to help you plan your exercise activities. Try using a specific timeframe (e.g. next week).

Your FIT Action Plan

Number of days I will do my exercise activities this week: _____

What days of the week will I do my activities? (please circle)

Mon   Tue   Wed   Thu   Fri   Sat   Sun

Specify what activities you will do, where, when, and for how long:

Day	Time	Activity	Duration	Intensity (0-100%)

Steps Using a Pedometer

Try using a pedometer to track the number of steps you take each day. Researchers suggest 10,000 steps each day bring maximum physical and mental health benefits.

	Mon	Tue	Wed	Thu	Fri	Sat	Sun
Steps (#)							
Goal met (Y/N)							

Track Your Action Plans as You Progress

Tracking will help you realize how effective your action plans are at helping you reach your goals and where you can make alterations to your plans.

How have your action plans been progressing?

1	2	3	4	5	6	7

not well at all   extremely well

How have your coping plans been working?

1	2	3	4	5	6	7

not well at all   extremely well

Modifications to Action Plans (if any):

Modifications to Coping Plans (if any):

Check-in on environmental cues and prompts you can use to exercise. Did you notice any cues in the environment that helped you exercise? Did you use any strategies to prompt yourself to move more (or sit less)?

Graphing Your Achievements

Plotting your achievements on a graph may be a helpful tool to visualize your progress. If you are tracking your daily steps with a pedometer, this graph will show your weekly and monthly progress.

Average Steps Taken Per Week

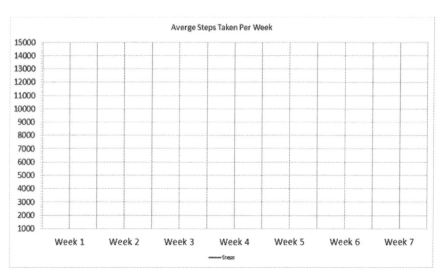

Step 8. Acknowledge Challenges and Stay Motivated

It is important to acknowledge that everyone will have lapses in their activity program for a few days or even a few weeks at some point for many different reasons. It is very important to think of these lapses as they are – temporary – and appreciate that you have the skills you need to get going again.

When a lapse happens, it important to look back at your goals and the reasons why you want to be an active person. Some of those will be the same and some will have changed because you have changed. Take stock of the improvements you have made. Make a plan, give yourself some positive self-talk, use your sources of support and get going again.

Your physical activity program, your cardiovascular fitness, and your strength are all works in progress. You will always be challenged (that's good!), and you will rise to the occasion.

Brainstorm a list of barriers or obstacles you have encountered so far when trying to reach your exercise goals.

Brainstorm a list of barriers or obstacles you anticipate encountering in the near future when trying to reach your exercise goals.

Some of the barriers are hard to change. What are some strategies you can use to overcome these obstacles?

Self-Compassion Tools

Sometimes challenges that keep us from meeting our goals are too difficult to cope with. When this happens, it is okay to take a break and treat yourself with kindness, sympathy, and compassion. Self-compassion writing exercises are particularly helpful if you are feeling negatively about current challenges or the challenges ahead.

Tool 1.[12] Think about a recent negative event where you experienced a failure that was difficult to cope with. This failure can be in regards to (i) your current appearance, body weight, shape, or size, or (ii) your fitness goals.

a) Briefly describe the event. What happened leading up to the event? Who was there? What happened during the event? What specific thoughts and actions occurred?

b) Write a paragraph expressing understanding, kindness and concern to yourself. Write as if you are communicating to a close friend in the same situation.

c) Describe the event in an objective and unemotional manner.

d) List ways in which other people may experience similar events.

Tool 2. To help you develop self-compassion, Dr. Kristin Neff has adapted one of Leslie Greenberg's gestalt exercises.[13] Neff says,

In this exercise, you will sit in different chairs to help get in touch with different, often conflicting parts of yourself, experiencing how each aspect feels in the present moment. To begin, put three empty chairs in a triangular arrangement. Next, think about an issue that often troubles you, and that often elicits harsh self-criticism. Designate one chair as the voice of your inner self-critic, one chair as the voice of the part of you that feels judged and criticized, and one chair as the voice of a wise, compassionate observer. You are going to be role-playing all three parts of yourself – you, you, and you. It may feel a bit silly at first, but you may be surprised at what comes out once you really start letting your feelings flow freely.

a) Think about your issue, and then sit in the chair of the self-critic. As you take your seat, express out loud what the self-critical part of you is thinking and feeling. For example, "I hate the fact that you're such a wimp and aren't self-assertive."

Notice the words and tone of voice used by the self-critical part of you, and also how it feels. Worried, angry, self-righteous, exasperated? Note what your body posture is like. Strong, rigid, upright? What emotions are coming up for you right now?

b) Take the chair of the criticized aspect of yourself. Try to get in touch with how you feel being criticized in this manner. Then verbalize how you feel, responding directly to your inner critic. For example, "I feel so hurt by you," or "I feel so unsupported." Just speak whatever comes into your mind. Again, notice the tone of your voice? Is it sad, discouraged, childlike, scared, helpless? What is your body posture like? Are you slumped, downward facing, frowning?

c) Conduct a dialogue between these two parts of yourself for a while, switching back and forth between the chair of the criticizer and the criticized. Really try to experience each aspect of yourself so each knows how the other feels. Allow each to fully express her views and be heard.

d) Now occupy the chair of the compassionate observer. Call upon your deepest wisdom, the wells of your caring concern, and address both the critic and the criticized. What does your compassionate self say to the critic, what insight does she have? For example, "You sound very much like your mother," or, "I see that you're really scared, and you're trying to help me so I don't mess up." What does your compassionate self say to the criticized part of yourself? For example, "It must be incredibly difficult to hear such harsh judgment day after day. I see that you're really hurting," or, "All you want is to be accepted for who you are." Try to relax, letting your heart soften and open. What words of compassion naturally spring forth? What is the tone of your voice? Tender, gentle, warm? What is your body posture like – balanced, centered, relaxed?

e) After the dialogue finishes (stop whenever it feels right), reflect upon what just happened. Do you have any new insights into how you treat yourself, where your patterns come from, new ways of thinking about the situation that are more productive and supportive? As you think about what you have learned, set your intention to relate to yourself in a kinder, healthier way in the future. A truce can be called in your inner war. Peace is possible. Your old habits of self-criticism don't need to rule you forever. What you need to do is listen to the voice that's already there, even if a bit hidden – your wise, compassionate self.

Physical Activity Contract

It is likely that you will face challenges when making a major lifestyle change. Research suggests that it can be helpful to make a *Physical Activity Contract* before beginning your journey and re-visit this contract any time you are facing difficulties meeting your goals. For example, there may be times over the next weeks and months when you may feel that it is almost impossible to follow the challenges. There will be times when you're tired, sad, stressed, angry, and maybe guilty or ashamed. It is during these times when you will need to revisit your contract most, to help remind yourself why you want to improve your health and well-being in the first place.

You will need to develop an attitude of "I can do this, I can work through any problems or barriers to achieve my goals." This attitude will help you live a longer, healthier life. Also, it is important to point out that there will be times when you slip up and forget your new physical activity strategies. Slip-ups are part of the process and to be expected. If there are many regular slip-ups, it will help to revisit your goals and refocus your attention. Throughout it is important to remember that sticking to your own plan will be worth it and you will feel so much better in the long run. It might not be easy, but it will be worth it. Your success is up to you. Your improved health is within your control. Keep telling yourself, "If it's going to be, it's up to me."

You can certainly seek help and ask for support – it is encouraged. However, no one can get you any healthier than you want to be and no one will be more committed than you are. You need your dedication, honesty, and commitment to succeed. If you feel that commitment, dedication, and honesty, let's work on your contract.

Physical Activity Contract

I, _____, am making an agreement to reach my goals of:

1.
2.
3.

I take responsibility for my physical activity – and I will make efforts towards achieving my goals. I will not criticize myself for any setbacks. I promise to learn from these setbacks. I realize that this process will not be easy, but I promise to try as best I can. I am ready for this change. During this challenge, I also promise to: (i) accept challenging times ahead; (ii) devote time to learn how to lead a healthier life, and I will use what I learn; (iii) remain focused, and get back on track when I slip up; (iv) I will not beat myself up. Instead, I promise to use this energy to re-motivate and re-engage my committed goals; (v) remember why I'm trying to become healthier, especially when I am tempted to give up; (vi) not let negative thoughts stop me from achieving my goals, and to give myself lots of positive feedback; (vii) try my best and strive to achieve my health goals despite setbacks and difficulties; (viii) enlist social support from friends and family to help keep me accountable but also to provide encouragement; (ix) sit down and re-read this contract when I feel challenged.

I am doing this challenge because I want to (circle, highlight, or underline all that apply):

- Feel better
- Enhance my memory and concentration
- Be able to move without pain
- Improve my sleep
- Improve my energy level

- Get sick less often
- Improve my mood
- Other

Signed: _____ Date:_____

Witness signature:_____

Congratulations on making the commitment to yourself. **Post this**!

Step 9. Recognize and Celebrate Your Achievements

Rewards

Rewards and positive self-talk are very important when you achieve your goals, and important for motivating you to get through challenging times. Make a plan on ways to reward yourself for reaching your goals. It is important that your rewards are positive, focus on your fitness, rather than appearance, and contribute to your overall health and well-being.

For example, a helpful reward may be deciding to buy yourself an exercise outfit that makes you feel good and comfortable, after completing your first 5K race. An example of a positive self-statement to follow: "I will feel so proud of myself for trying something new and pushing through the challenging times."

Now it's your turn. Complete your goals, positive self-statement, and planned rewards. When you complete your goal, add in the date you achieved it and follow through with your reward.

Goal 1:
Positive self-statement for future you:

Planned Reward:
Date achieved:

Goal 2:
Positive self-statement for future you:

Planned Reward:
Date achieved:

Goal 3:
Positive self-statement for future you:

Planned Reward:
Date achieved:

Step 10. Assess Your Results; Imagine the Possibilities

Goal Checkup

One of the best ways to keep yourself focused and determined to improve your activity levels is to regularly check up on how far you have come in changing your behavior. The purpose of this exercise is to examine one of your past goals, how you progressed, and things that helped you reach your goal, or problems that you encountered. **Write down your goal here**:

How would you rate your progress towards that goal? **Circle the number that best represents your progress towards your goal.** For example, if you completely met your goal, circle 100%. However, if you were able to make it halfway to your goal, circle 50%.

| 0% | 25% | 50% | 75% | 100% |

When thinking about progress towards your goal, it is important to be aware of things that helped you and things that made it difficult. **Write down things that helped you progress towards your goal and areas where you could use some suggestions or new options:**

Based on this writing exercise, **create a new goal** that will help you overcome your challenges and barriers:

About Our Contributors

Kirsten Bedard, Bsc Nutrition, ACE

Kirsten Bedard is one of Canada's most knowledgeable nutrition and exercise coaches. She is the founder of Ladylean. Kirsten helps her clients implement science-based strategies to fuel their bodies effectively, and by doing so they maximize mental and physical performance – at work and at play. She has integrated her vast and precise knowledge of food chemistry, exercise science, and the workings of the body into a clear and simple approach to eating and exercise. Her clients have transformed their lives. Kirsten's first book, *Read This Before You Diet* (forthcoming), is a direct, no-nonsense, guide to three basic principles of weight loss.

Debra Joy Eklove, BCom, MSc, CAE

Debra is a member of the board of directors of **The Art of Living Foundation Canada**,* and past president. Her passion is improving people's lives and welfare. She has done this work as a not-for-profit manager, as an energy medicine practitioner, and as a singer. Her CD of original music is called *A Process to Heart*. Debra has a bachelor of commerce degree from McGill University, a masters in economics from the London School of Economics, is a Certified Association Manager, an Ayurveda nutrition consultant, and teacher of TLEX and The Art of Living Happiness Programs.

Eva Pila, MSc, PhD candidate, Exercise Science, University of Toronto

Eva is currently a PhD candidate in health and exercise psychology at the University of Toronto. Eva completed her undergraduate degree at McMaster University and her master's degree at both McGill University and the University of Toronto. Her research focuses on body image concerns in at-risk populations, including adolescent girls and women with chronic illness. Her research aims to better understand how women experience self-consciousness around the body, and how these feelings can impact their exercise and nutrition choices and motivation. Since high school, Eva has been deeply involved with various community and health groups to promote healthy, active living and positive body image. The overall goal of her research and community involvement is to promote compassionate body image, self-worth, and overall well-being in girls and women.

Catherine M. Sabiston, Canada Research Chair, Associate Professor, University of Toronto

Dr. Catherine Sabiston holds a Canada Research Chair in Physical Activity and Mental Health and is an associate professor of exercise and health psychology in the Faculty of Kinesiology and Physical Education at the University of Toronto. Catherine has been studying challenges associated with body image, women's health, and physical activity for over fifteen years. She has held over $15 million in funding for her research, has published 140 research articles and has given over 300 presentations. For this work, she has received numerous professional awards. In addition to her research, Catherine has given many community talks and workshops at schools, and has been a mental health consultant for women diagnosed with breast cancer.

Nayna Trehan, BCom

Nayna is a business graduate from Royal Roads University. She is an **Art of Living Foundation*** teacher, through which she helps people unlock their true potential using ancient practices of yoga, meditation, and breathing exercises. She is also passionate about helping people live a healthier and more mindful life through the knowledge of ayurveda, a system of natural health and wellness.

* The Art of Living Foundation[14]

Operating in over 150 countries, The Art of Living Foundation (AOLF) is a volunteer-run non-profit, educational, and humanitarian organization founded in 1981 by the world-renowned humanitarian and spiritual leader, an ambassador of peace and human values, Sri Sri Ravi Shankar. All of AOLF's programs are guided by Sri Sri's philosophy: "Unless we have a stress-free mind and a violence-free society, we cannot achieve world peace."

AOLF offers educational and self-development programs and tools to help eliminate stress and foster deep profound inner peace, happiness, and well-being for all individuals. These programs include breathing techniques, meditation, yoga, and practical wisdom for daily living. They have helped millions around the world transform their lives regardless of their background, culture, or traditions.

Working in collaboration with The International Association of Human Values, AOLF has been part of humanitarian projects and service initiatives. These include conflict resolution programs, disaster relief, sustainable rural development, empowerment of women, prisoner rehabilitation, education for underprivileged children, and environmental sustainability.

About the Authors

Susan Sommers

Born in New Jersey, Susan Sommers is one of Canada's best-known authors and experts in marketing and media relations, and the author of four books. Her book *Power Source for Women: Proven Fitness Strategies, Tools, and Success Stories for Women 45+* was co-authored with Theresa Dugwell in 2010.

Susan's vision for physical and mental fitness emerged from her own long-standing issues and struggles with weight-cycling and body image. She thus brings unique personal inspiration to her quest to mentor and educate women about the life-changing impact of a proper program of personal health and fitness. She has delivered inspirational workshops related to women's fitness and health throughout in Canada and in the United States.

Susan's perspective took a fundamental shift in 2002 when she began to walk and jog, as a new Toronto YMCA member, at the age of fifty-eight. In 2005 and 2007, Susan completed two full marathons in Toronto, walking and jogging for over seven hours. Over the past twelve years, Susan has completed thirty races, from 5Ks to marathons, started to lap swim, and committed to meditation.

Susan has been featured on television and radio shows and in a variety of fitness and women's magazines, including the LIVESTRONG blog, *The Globe and Mail* newspaper, *Canadian*

Running magazine, *Active Adult* magazine, *Thornhill Post*, Rogers *Daytime Toronto*, and impowerage.com.

A dynamic speaker, Susan was a featured speaker at an International Women's Day Celebration in Jaipur, India, in March 2015. As a keynote speaker, she participated in a number of fundraising events, including Power of the Purse and Joy of Aging. She is appreciated for her motivational keynotes and seminars, which include LuluLemon Athletica, Running Room, and Lole. She was the inaugural speaker for the YMCA Women's Speaker Series on defining achievement in personal fitness.

Susan believes in motivating girls and boys to appreciate and embrace their bodies through fitness. She and her nine-year-old granddaughter have participated in Girls on the Run, an annual non-competitive 5K event that aims to educate and prepare girls for a lifetime of self-respect and healthy living. They have also participated in Kiwanis fundraising events with Susan's husband Peter, who is a two-time Boston Marathoner. Her other two granddaughters compete in sports on Vancouver Island and her three grandsons are talented hockey players.

Susan established her own communications company in 1982 (Susan Sommers + Associates) and, since then, she has authored four books on marketing and media relations. She has taught and lectured extensively in universities and at conferences across Canada and has been teaching at University of Toronto, Continuing Studies, since 1992.

Susan is a tour leader for the Women's Travel Network.

Theresa Dugwell

Theresa Dugwell is President of PsyMetrics Professional Services and has been a coach and mentor for women of all ages. She is strongly involved in the growth of female entrepreneurship. She consults with clinics of all health modalities to help rejuvenate their environments and patient relationships.

Theresa is a past member of the Canadian Psychological Association, American Psychological Association, and Ontario Association of Consultants, Counsellors, Psychometrists and Psychotherapists, and past volunteer chair for the Association of Biofeedback and Psychophysiology. She is a certified life skills coach and mind-body fitness coach, a certified spinning and fitness instructor specialist, and has the Canadian fitness professionals certification. She is also one of the first volunteers to be selected to train as a YMCA Canadian trainer/facilitator for fitness instructors.

Theresa holds three Guinness World Records for running the greatest distance in twelve hours on a treadmill in the overall and women's category. She has completed twenty-one marathons and currently trains with Olympic gold medalist Mark McKoy. Her dream is to try out for the masters provincial qualifying races in the 100-meter distance in 2016 – with a big audacious goal of competing in the world masters one day.

Theresa is a workshop facilitator and speaker, who has created and delivered workshops on emotional intelligence in the work place, creativity and self-esteem, developing your running style, and the psychophysiology of the stress response.

As an active volunteer at the North York YMCA since 2005, Theresa has received the Volunteer of the Year Award, created events for International Women's Day, and organized the Breakfast of Champions fundraisers. She developed a monthly workshop series, "Celebrating Women," to celebrate the successes and obstacles of women who are YMCA members. Theresa was part of the team that created the Megathon, a yearly fundraising event that is celebrated for twelve hours on the first Saturday of every March throughout all of the YMCA's in the Greater Toronto Area. It is one of the YMCA's biggest fundraisers and has helped many families get active and build community. She has also represented the North York YMCA Leadership Council as Chair.

Theresa is a founding member of the North York YMCA Women's Fund, Buy a Brick, Build a Life Campaign, which assisted women and children in shelters by providing them with YMCA memberships to open up a world of community, health, and fitness during a transitional period.

Theresa is co-author of *Power Source for Women: Proven Fitness Strategies, Tools, and Success Stories for Women 45+.*

Notes and Bibliography

1   Susan Sommers and Theresa Dugwell, *Power Source for Women: Proven Fitness Strategies, Tools, and Success Stories for Women 45+.* (Toronto: BPS Books, 2010).

2   Kirsten Bedard, *Read This Before You Diet.* (Forthcoming). Find out more about Kirsten Bedard's work at www.ladylean.com.

3   Olga Kotelko, *The O.K. Way to a Healthy and Happy Life.* (Victoria, BC: FriesenPress, 2014).

4   Bruce Grierson, *What Makes Olga Run? The Mystery of the 90-Something Track Star, and What She Can Teach Us About Living Longer, Happier Lives.* (Toronto: Vintage Canada, 2014).

5   Kathrine Switzer, *Marathon Woman: Running the Race to Revolutionize Women's Sports.* (Cambridge, MA: Da Capo Press, 2009); Kathrine Switzer, *Running and Walking for Women Over 40.* (New York: St. Martin's Griffin, 1998); Kathrine Switzer and Roger Robinson, *26.2 Marathon Stories.* (New York: Vhps Rodale, 2006).

6   Margaret Webb, *Older, Faster, Stronger* (New York: Rodale Books, 2014).

7   Bruce Grierson, *What Makes Olga Run?*

8   Developed in the Health Behaviour and Emotion Lab at University of Toronto.

9   Adapted from "Advantages and Disadvantages of Change." *Cognitive Behavioural Therapy Self-Help Resources* website. Accessed in January 2016. http://www.getselfhelp.co.uk/docs/Change.pdf

10 Adapted from Jack M. Richman, Lawrence B. Rosenfeld, and Charles J. Hardy. "The Social Support Survey: A Validation Study

of a Clinical Measure of the Social Support Process." *Research on Social Work Practice* 3 (1993): 288.

[11] Adapted from Carol Vivyan, 2010. "Mood Diary." *Cognitive Behavioural Therapy Self-Help Resources* website. Accessed in January 2016. http://www.getselfhelp.co.uk/docs/MoodDiary2.pdf.

[12] Adapted from Kristin Neff, *Self-Compassion* website. Accessed in January 2016. http://self-compassion.org; and from A.D. Mosewich, P.R.E. Crocker, K.C. Kowalski, and A. DeLongis, "Applying self-compassion in sport: An intervention with women athletes." *Journal of Sport and Exercise Psychology* 35 (2013): 514-524.

[13] Kristin Neff, "Exercise 4: The criticizer, the criticized, and the compassionate observer." *Self-Compassion* website. Accessed in January 2016. http://self-compassion.org/ exercise-4-criticizer-criticized-compassionate-observer/

[14] Learn more about The Art of Living Foundation at www.artofliving. org and about the founder at www.srisriravishankar.org.